OUT OF THE SHADOWS

OUT OF THE SHADOWS

How London gay life changed
for the better after the Act

A History of the pioneering London gay groups
and organisations, 1967–2000

With a Foreword by Michael Cashman MEP

Editor: Tony Walton
Copy Editor: Ross Burgess
Technical Editor: Clive Clareton

Bona Street Press

Out of the Shadows
Edited by Tony Walton

First published 2010 by Bona Street Press,
BM Box 7128, London WC1N 3XX

Reprinted with minor corrections, 2011

www.slago.org.uk/oots.htm

ISBN 978-0-9566091-0-6

Set in Garamond and Nimrod MT

50% of profits will be donated to the Terrence Higgins Trust and the Peter Tatchell Human Rights Fund

CONTENTS

Contents

List of illustrations ... iv
Foreword by Michael Cashman MEP ... vii
Acknowledgements ... viii
Editor's Introduction ... 1
1 The St Katharine's (SK) Group 1968–1994 ... 3
2 London Gay Liberation Front (GLF) 1970–1974 ... 12
3 CHE in London 1971– ... 30
4 The London Monday Group 1971– ... 38
5 The Marypad Group 1971– ... 46
6 The Croydon Group 1971– ... 49
7 Annual Events in London ... 59
8 Harrow Group 1972– ... 65
9 Jewish Groups 1972– ... 68
10 The Wandsworth-Richmond Group 1972–1983 ... 70
11 London Friend 1972– ... 77
12 The Lewisham Groups 1972–1985 ... 86
13 A Miscellany, including ... 92
    Ealing Gay Group (EGG) 1980– ... 92
    Octopus Group 1982– ... 93
    The Walking Group ... 93
    Pimpernel 1984–99 ... 93
    Naturist Groups ... 94
14 The Streatham Group 1972–1986 ... 95
15 Icebreakers 1973–c.1984 ... 102
16 Quest 1973– ... 104
17 WAGS (Wimbledon Area Gay Society) 1973–1995 ... 111
18 Metropolitan Community Church, London 1973– ... 125
19 Gay Teachers and Schools OUT 1974– ... 130
20 The Transport Group 1974– ... 144
21 Bexley and Bromley Gay Groups 1974–2001 ... 152
22 CHE Youth Group 1974–c.1980 ... 160
23 The Southwark-Lambeth Group 1976–1980 ... 169
24 The Kingston Group 1976–2001 ... 175

iii

List of illustrations

Foreword by Michael Cashman MEP

I was greatly interested when I heard about *Out of the Shadows* and I read it with anticipation.

It charts an eye-popping account of the explosion of activity in London which followed the change in the law in 1967. The years preceding this date were grim indeed for many gay people and this legislation was nothing short of life-transforming.

I am writing this introduction during LGBT History Month 2010 and I feel that this London story makes an especially useful contribution to that history. The story of the very first UK gay group ever (St Katharine's in East London), together with the accounts of the other various groups across the capital, is an important one. There is much in this book which has not been previously put to paper and that is why it forms a valuable historical record.

I have much pleasure in commending all the various accounts, contributed by many different individuals, to your reading.

Michael Cashman

Acknowledgements

A huge number of people have contributed to this book but special acknowledgements and thanks are due to the following for allowing us to put in extracts from their books (details of the books themselves are given in the Bibliography at the end):

- Rex Batten
- Lisa Power
- Jeffrey Weeks.

Our front cover photograph is taken, with permission, from Lisa Power's book.

The photographs of Sue Sanders and Paul Patrick in Chapter 19 are reproduced from Wikipedia, the Free Encyclopedia, under the Creative Commons Attribution ShareAlike 3.0 licence.

Also thanks to Peter Tatchell for permission to use an article first published in *Boyz* Magazine (18 June 2009) and again in *All God's Children* (LGCM's magazine, July 2009).

Thanks to Robert Liston who contributed very many of the photographs in this book.

Also thanks to Duncan Strivens and Laurie Smith for permission for their Bromley photos to be included and to an anonymous member of SLG for permission for his Kingston group cartoons to be used.

And finally thanks to Malcolm King for the final proof-read, picking up errors that the rest of us had failed to notice.

Editor's Introduction

In 2007 the 3F group of LGCM celebrated its thirtieth anniversary. We decided to put together a short pamphlet outlining the history of the group, and therefore contacted those who had run the group in the past, asking for their recollections.

One of the people we contacted was Rev Malcolm Johnson who had been Rector of St Botolph's, Aldgate when the group started there. It occurred to me almost straight away that Malcolm had also been a key figure in the setting up of a more important group, historically speaking, namely St Katharine's—the very first UK gay group to have come into being after the change of the law in 1967. So we decided to ask Malcolm for his recollections of both the groups he had been involved with, and to have two separate chapters on the two groups in the pamphlet.

Later several people suggested that the recollections in the book were so valuable as a part of LGBT history that they should be made into a proper book, with the other London groups 1967–2000 included too. It was felt a record should be kept of how the various groups and organisations had established themselves in the thirty years after the passing of the Act, and most especially during the key years of the 1970s. These were years in which gay lives had indeed been greatly changed for the better but which, at least at the local group level, have often been left unrecorded. This book is the result of those suggestions.

The decision was taken to restrict it mainly to London, as it would have been a huge project to cover the history of all the groups across the country, although we've included some groups which were based in London but had activities outside.

We also decided not to include the history of the separate groups for women and those for transsexuals as we felt they would prefer to write their own histories, although it's worth noting that almost all the London groups mentioned in the book were inclusive in their early days and had many lesbian members. Unfortunately probably only in the cases of Metropolitan Community Church and Schools OUT was there ever something approaching equality of numbers. Because women were in such a minority in the others it was perhaps inevitable they would form their own groups, with the result that over the years many "mixed" groups have become predominantly male in membership.

I would like to thank all those many individuals who have contributed with their memories and comments. With so many contributing there are bound to be differences of opinion, and indeed there are bound to be errors in the book—since we are relying on people's memories of a period of sometimes more than forty years ago. But for all its weaknesses, we feel the effort has been hugely worthwhile in the recording at local level of what must have been the most transforming thirty years in UK gay history. We hope you will enjoy reading all the different accounts.

Any book that tries to record a period of history for the first time will make errors and leave out some important points. As we go to press, new information is arriving. Amendments and corrections will be added to the website of the Surrey and London Association of Gay Organisations, SLAGO, **www.slago.org.uk/oots.htm**. Please e-mail **info@slago.org.uk** if you can offer more information, corrections or pictures from the past (in the case of pictures, you may need to get permission from whoever owns the copyright).

Tony Walton

Chapter One
The SK Group 1968–1994

St Katharine's group was formed in the autumn of 1968, just a year after the Act went through Parliament decriminalising homosexuality.

The change in the law had been brought about by the Wolfenden Report of 1957, but little notice had been taken of Wolfenden at first, so it was mainly the work of the Albany Trust and of the Homosexual Law Reform Society (the two organisations were run by the same people, and notably the late Antony Grey) which got the law finally changed in 1967. Thus it had taken a whole ten years of effort to get the recommendations of Wolfenden put into practice!

The Albany Trust held a conference in Wychcroft in Surrey in July 1968 to decide the way ahead. Three members—Malcolm Johnson[1], Andrew Henderson[2] and Christopher Spence[3]—offered to start a social group for gay men, and Father Augustine Hoey offered the common room at the Royal Foundation. The Foundation of St Katharine's was an Anglican community committed to social justice, like its role model Trevor Huddleston (Malcolm Johnson has been told that the Queen Mother, who was the Patron of the Foundation, agreed to this). So, as Richard Kirker has pointed out, it was a wonderful thing that the SK group was in premises owned and managed by the people of the community who gave it their full, if discreet, backing.

In the year following de-criminalisation the Albany Trust (with an office at 32 Shaftesbury Avenue) had been almost bombarded with gay people wanting as it were "to get on to the scene". They had led closeted

---

[1] Malcolm Johnson was at the time Chaplain at Queen Mary College London, went on to become Rector of St Botolph's Aldgate, and later still was master of St Katharine's itself.

[2] Andrew Henderson is a priest, now retired. He was Director of Social Services for Kensington and Chelsea.

[3] Christopher Spence is a layman and was then PA to Selwyn Lloyd MP. Andrew and Christopher founded the London Lighthouse for people with AIDS.

lives because it had all been against the law and they had not been lucky enough to make contact with other gay people or to form friendships with similarly minded people. It had become obvious that some kind of meeting place must be set up to cater for the social needs of this large number.

The answer was to be the formation of the St Katharine's Group, and no one was ever turned away, either at this stage or later, in the history of SK.

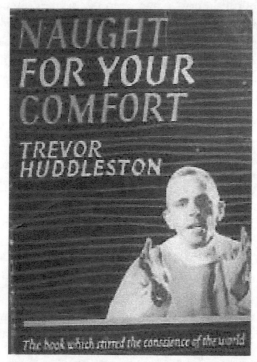

Trevor Huddleston's most famous book

The Trust realised that social facilities for gays and lesbians had been very lacking. There were indeed so-called "gay clubs", technically just late-night drinking clubs with a gay clientele, but these were not to the taste of many gay people for various reasons—they were often of a commercial, predatory nature. They were associated in many gays' minds with one-night stands and blackmail, and although the threat of the latter had disappeared with de-criminalisation in theory, the image tended to remain. (We say "in theory" because people like gay teachers were still in a vulnerable position—see Bill Boyd's story on page 6).

Having a place like St Katharine's to meet was the most wonderful bonus and it seemed like the answer to prayer. The group was called SK since obviously it met at St Katharine's, although the name was also useful as in the early very fearful days it deliberately gave no clue to the purpose of the organisation.

Members were referred mainly by Doreen Cordell who was the counsellor of the Trust, and Malcolm still has her referral letters which were very detailed. Doreen was almost considered a saint by many of the gay men who had been to see her. She died in about 1990 and Andrew Henderson recollects how her funeral was attended by an unusually varied group of people—scouts and guides, alongside gays from the SK group, in addition to several TVs and TSs since she was an expert in that field.

The Royal Foundation of St Katharine's as it is now (2007)

We usually met at St Katharine's on Saturday evenings. For the first year we wondered if we would be raided by the police and a deliberately boring social work style hand-out was prepared, saying that we were helping lonely homosexuals who had come for counselling. Meetings began in the autumn of 1968 and we all wore smart clothes, someone played the piano and there was an improving talk for about thirty minutes. The emphasis was on fostering sincere friendships and relationships.

The whole thing was conducted with great care and caution in a way which seems slightly laughable now nearly forty years on, but you must remember everyone had grown up in an atmosphere of complete illegality and secrecy. So potential members had to go through a vetting procedure to make sure they understood what it was about and to tell them the rules. Codes of behaviour were enforced and the existence of the group was kept in the early days very secret.

The Bad Old Days

As we say, all of this SK secrecy seems a bit ridiculous now, but perhaps if we tell you the story of a teacher, Bill Boyd, now a member of South London Gays, you will see how necessary and understandable the whole thing was.

Bill had taken a job in a school near Rotherham and used to visit the nearest pub in which gays tended to congregate for social contact. It was the custom for gays in this pub to be invited back after closing time to an individual's flat, and on one occasion Bill invited them all back to his place. Being a summer evening they went out into the garden and would just be enjoying the friendly socialising that the SK group used to in the safety of the Foundation.

During the course of the evening, however, an irate neighbour knocked on the door to complain, not about the noise but about the fact that they were all MEN! He said he had seen some of them cuddling or kissing and, almost beside himself with rage, expressed the opinion that they were—and he had difficulty saying the word, being so disgusted and shocked, but finally managing to mouth it—"HOMO-SEXUALS!"

Sadly the matter didn't end there, since the neighbour reported Bill to the headmaster of the local school in which he was teaching. The headmaster summoned Bill into his room and told him that, with great regret, he had no option but to ask him to leave. The date this all happened? 1969—two years after the change in the law and one year after the start of SK.

Something now from the editor:

My thanks to Bill for letting us include the last story. I wanted also to tell you about Terry Noble, not just because he was an occasional member of SK, but because of the whole theme of this book which is how gays were radically changing from one epoch into the next. Terry belonged to the *old* epoch, and he was one of those many gays who said that in some ways he preferred things as they had been before. They'd often tell us we must not "rock the boat" by being too open and too bold!

I used to ask Terry about how things used to be—as the gay scene before the passing of the Act was something I knew nothing about, having only come onto the scene through SK in October 1968. In fact Terry Noble loved talking about the old days: it all used to work very well, he said, so long as you got into "the Old Queens' Tea Parties." An older gay would meet a younger one (in a cottage or whatever) and would invite him round for Sunday afternoon tea at his house—where a quite large gathering of mixed ages would assemble.

Another member of SK, Doug Randall, used to tell me that he regarded SK as a kind of escape from the "real" gay scene, which to him had always meant places like the William IV in Hampstead and the Rockingham Club in the West End, which he had been lucky enough to find out about.

Of course both Terry and Doug would freely have admitted that, however good it had been for those on the "inside", there were huge numbers of gay people—maybe three out of four, even in London?—who knew absolutely nothing about the tea parties or the Rockingham. (And Bill Boyd's story confirms that even the most relaxed gatherings could run into trouble). Most gay people led completely isolated lives in the shadows and only got an occasional grope in the darkness—metaphorical or literal.

To reinforce the above: since we wrote and first published this SK chapter in 2007, an interesting piece of evidence has come to light. Geoff of Croydon Friend has told us he remembers how one evening in about 1969 or 1970 the St Katharine's group *was* raided by the police—they were looking for someone whom they wanted to arrest and they asked a lot of questions, Geoff remembers. They finally took someone away, and everyone else was understandably left very shaken.

Improving Lives

SK, which started in October 1968, was definitely the first established gay group in the UK, as it was two or three years before GLF arrived, and three to five years before the network of CHE groups would be set up on a local basis across the country. Many of the people attending SK had had no gay social contact before, having led lives of isolation. The group by its nature meant that everyone could be at ease and could mingle freely in an atmosphere of safety and relaxation with other gay people—assuming there was no police raid!

The Foundation was right by the side of what is now Limehouse Station on the Docklands Light Railway (you can peer down into the Foundation as you travel along it), but in those days it was not easy to get to by public transport—most people had to get the underground to Aldgate or Aldgate East and then wait for the infrequent Saturday evening bus service along Commercial Road.

After a year we ran out of subjects to discuss, and also we had so many members that we moved from the common room into the small hall. An informal bar was organised and it was suggested after a while that we should have dancing too; in fact some people voted against this and so, because the emphasis was always on keeping everyone happy, we decided to have dancing on alternate weeks only!

The largest of the three rooms had a stage and we used it for parties. Disco parties were held on special occasions like Christmas and New Year's Eve, and for those we would use the large, rather barn-like hall next door to the usual small hall where we met. (The common room is still there but the two halls have been pulled down and re-developed).

On one occasion we were entertained in the large hall by a then little known drag duo called Hinge and Bracket, who later became celebrities with their own TV show called "Dear Ladies."

One of the very few rules of the group was that you should never refuse if anyone asked you to dance! Very sensible. Once we had "Dancing for the Deaconesses" and gave a large sum to the nuns who lived and worked at the Foundation as well as some monks. The sisters often came along to functions and were very popular, and one Master, Father Jack

Guinness, was a member too. (We remember how lots of SK members attended his funeral).

A guest system was later adopted to make the whole system less rigid. The younger members tended to think that the whole thing was a bit too formal in its attitude—one committee member in charge of membership was given the nickname of "Auntie" for this reason, although the teasing was always good natured.

Commercial Road area, close to the Foundation
The White Swan is now a gay pub

For many people the whole thing, in the early days, was a complete eye-opener on the gay world and you'd hear people saying "Well I'm blowed, I never realised that (whoever) was queer!" and so on. And yes, we did always use the word "queer" for each other, rather than "gay", back in the sixties. On one occasion a committee member named Stanley spoke to us in about 1970 about "the gay bars" of New York and for some of us it was the first time we had heard the word used in that way.

Others were desperate to know where these renowned queer pubs of London actually were. One person was amazed to find he had been driving past the William IV in Hampstead and the Black Cap in Camden Town many times without realising that they were two of the best known.

Remember it had been *completely impossible* to get information in those days, unless you were lucky enough to meet the right people.

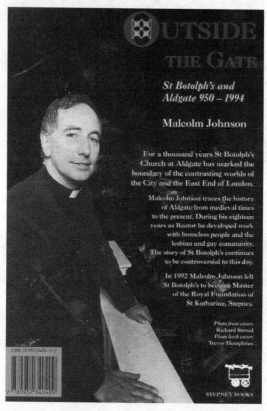

Outside the Gate by Malcolm Johnson, one of the founders of SK

Needing a break from East London, we would sometimes go en masse to a pub in the West End. Once, in about February 1969, we arranged to meet in a straight pub in Berwick Street called the Green Man, and a very large group of us enjoyed a jolly evening together. As we had practically taken over the whole bar we wondered seriously if a new gay pub was about to be born. But it wasn't—sadly. At the same evening one illustrious member of the group, Bill Mackrell, explained he was shortly taking over as the warden of a Unitarian hostel in Albert Street, Camden Town, not far from the Black Cap. He said how great it would be if some members of SK joined him there as residents—and at least one did.

After a few years we had women members too. Malcolm also used to organise a "Young Group" of SK for the under thirties to try to cater for the younger members, and on Fridays he would take them to the West End where there were still a few gay clubs, their favourite one being the Rehearsal in Piccadilly.

The emphasis throughout the gay community was, for several years following 1967, on us gays organising things for ourselves, and we often felt that these community based efforts were better than the commercial ones. Only during the eighties did the commercial sector take over pretty well everything and was it reluctantly accepted that *maybe* they did it better.

Many other gay organisations were already starting to spring up. Once that happened it was inevitable that the numbers at SK would decline—especially since, as we have mentioned, public transport to Limehouse was in those days so poor. Leslie recalls, however, that even in the last few years special events were well-attended—sometimes up to 150. There would be parties for Hallowe'en and the New Year, with the 25th birthday party in October 1993 being particularly well supported.

Of course we had our share of bereavements in those sad days in the eighties when HIV/AIDS amongst gays was at its height, but we just kept on going, even though numbers for various reasons were declining.

In 1994 the Foundation announced that the buildings were to be partly demolished and redeveloped, and it was felt that with diminished numbers there was no point in continuing the group.

But even today SK is considered a "gay social milestone" or a "gay social godsend" which brought happiness to many in the bleak atmosphere of the late sixties and who now have very fond memories of it. They remember particularly the lasting friendships which were formed.

Richard Kirker has suggested that a blue plaque should be put up outside the Royal Foundation to commemorate the SK Group.

We are very grateful to Andrew Henderson, Malcolm Johnson and Leslie Smith for giving their recollections of the SK group.

Chapter Two

London Gay Liberation Front (GLF) 1970–1974

Peter Tatchell recalls the idealism and passion of the pioneering London Gay Liberation Front of the early 1970s.

From victims to victors

We've come a long way baby. After a campaign that began five decades ago, the explicit homophobia of English criminal law finally ended in 2003. The Sexual Offences Act was passed that year. It abolished the gay-only sex crime of 'gross indecency'—the law used to jail Oscar Wilde in 1895.

He wasn't the only victim. It is estimated that more than 50,000 gay and bisexual men were convicted of 'gross indecency' during the 118 years it was on the statute books. The law against "buggery" (anal sex)—which dated back to the 1500s—was repealed in the same legislation, ensuring non-discrimination in the penal code from the first time in almost 500 years.

Also in 2003, discrimination against queers in the workplace was finally outlawed following a campaign that took 30 years. When gay employee Tony Whitehead was sacked from British Home Stores in 1974 he lacked any legal redress. Today, employers can no longer sack queers at will. At long last, lesbians, gays and bisexuals have the same job protection that was given to black people in 1967.

How did we progress from the bad old days of rampant persecution to what is now a significant degree of social acceptance? What enabled our queer nation to finally start gaining recognition, respect and rights?

The formation of the Gay Liberation Front in London in 1970 was, arguably, the beginning of the modern movement for queer human rights in Britain. Together with thousands of other gays and lesbians, I was part of GLF's queer uprising.

There were earlier, courageous movements, including the Homosexual Law Reform Society and the North West Homosexual Law Reform Committee, which later became the Campaign for Homosexual Equality. I recall with admiration the efforts of trail-blazers like Allan Horsfall, Antony Grey, Jackie Forster and Griff Vaughan Williams.

But GLF was the explosion that ignited a firestorm. It transformed the mind of queer Britain forever—replacing shame with pride, and fear with defiance.

Protest, not apology

GLF did not plead for reform; it demanded change. Feisty, radical and uncompromising, our goal was the transformation of straight society. GLF set the agenda for all the gains of the last three decades.

Rejecting the often closeted, seemingly apologetic pleas for tolerance voiced by many law reformers in the 1950s and 60s, GLF activists were out and proud. We demanded a gay-positive and sex-affirmative society, where everyone could love whoever they wanted, without guilt, stigma or discrimination.

Inspired by GLF's freedom cry, for the first time in history thousands of queers stopped hiding their sexuality and suffering in silence. No longer prepared to remain passive victims of injustice, we came out and marched with pride for gay liberation.

GLF's unique style of political campaigning was "protest as performance". Theatrical, imaginative, camp, daring and witty, it promoted the queer rights message in entertaining ways that caught people's attention. There were spirited agitprop media stunts and street theatre spectaculars, like the raid on Harley Street in protest at the "psycho Nazis" in the psychiatric profession who said homosexuality was a mental illness. These novel protest methods helped raise public awareness of the institutional homophobia that was wrecking our lives.

GLF put fun into politics. A 12-foot papier-mâché cucumber was delivered to the offices of Pan Books in protest at Dr David Reuben's homophobic book, *Everything You Always Wanted To Know About Sex*, which suggested that gay men were obsessed with shoving vegetables up their bums.

When Mary Whitehouse began her crusade against the "moral pollution" of the "permissive society" (homosexuality, abortion and pornography), GLF disrupted her launch rally at Central Hall Westminster with mice, whistles and kissing nuns.

There were also serious civil disobedience protests, modelled on the tactics of Mahatma Gandhi and Martin Luther King; including sit-ins in pubs, like the Chepstow in west London which refused to serve "poofs" and "lezzos".

Realising straight men oppress both women and gays, GLF allied itself with women's liberation movement. The 1971 Miss World contest at the Royal Albert Hall was upstaged by an alternative pageant outside the main entrance, featuring the drag queens Miss Used, Miss Conceived and Miss Treated. In protest at global hunger and Britain's war in Ireland, there were also guest appearances by Miss Ulster, swathed in bloody bandages, and by a starving, emaciated Miss Bangladesh.

These protests grabbed the headlines and put queer issues on the public agenda, provoking debate and helping change homophobic attitudes.

Most importantly, the sight of queers fighting back against our persecutors dispelled forever the idea that straight society could walk all over us with impunity. This transformation from victim to victor was emotionally uplifting for millions of previously downtrodden and downcast queers. It helped banish our internalised shame, repairing much of mental damage done to us by centuries of homophobia.

Through GLF we became the first queer generation to cast off the stigma and self-hate that had burdened us for over 2,000 years. The result?

We became happier, more confident people, determined to assert our rights and unafraid to challenge even the most powerful homophobes.

The Old World Order

Given the recent strides made by our community, it is easy to forget how bad things were just over three decades ago. Back then, it was not uncommon for lesbians and gay men to be sacked from their jobs, arrested for kissing in the street, evicted by homophobic landlords, and denied custody of their children by court order.

In the movies, if we featured at all, we were ridiculed as limp-wristed queens and demonised as psychopathic dykes. The only gay people who featured in the news were mass murderers, spies and child abusers. We were the enemy within.

Queer bashing was rife, but largely ignored by the police and media. Cruising and cottaging were treated as major sex crimes, with constant raids. The police also periodically targeted gay clubs and bars. Owners were charged with "keeping a disorderly house" and patrons were arrested for "licentious dancing".

At that time, there were no openly gay public figures, no sympathetic gay characters on television, and no gay switchboards or help-lines for those in need.

No wonder there was so much queer self-loathing, depression, alcoholism and suicide. Many gays were ashamed and wished they were straight—or dead. Some went to doctors to get "cured". Others were sentenced by the courts to undergo "treatment". Leading psychologists, such as Professor Hans Eysenck, advocated electric-shock aversion therapy to turn gay people straight.

We had a huge battle on our hands. Centuries of homophobia dictated that lesbian and gay people were mad, sad and very, very bad. Undaunted, GLF turned convention on its head, declaring: "Gay Is Good!" These three words, spray-painted all over London, signalled a revolution in queer consciousness.

In those days it was deemed outrageous to suggest there was anything good about being gay. Even liberal-minded heterosexuals mostly supported gay law reform out of sympathy and pity. Many were aghast when GLF proclaimed: "2-4-6-8! Gay is just as good as straight!" This simple slogan had a huge impact. It psychologically empowered queers everywhere, but it frightened the life out of smug, arrogant heterosexuals who had always assumed they were superior. Unbowed by more than two millennia of heterosexual dictatorship, we dared to question straight supremacism, likening it to racism and misogyny.

While the church and state viewed homosexuality as a social problem, we argued the real problem was society's homophobia. Instead of gays having to justify their existence, GLF demanded that gay-haters justify their bigotry.

In the 30-plus years since GLF first sparked queer rebellion there have been many advances. The repeal of homophobic legislation has included equalising the age of consent, ending the ban on homosexuals in the military and legalising gay adoption and civil partnerships. Gay people are more visible than ever before, with openly gay politicians, police, priests and pop stars.

Public attitudes are much more accepting. Positive queer images and characters abound on television. Companies run gay-themed adverts and political parties bid for the queer vote. The police have got tougher on homophobic hate crimes (except, very notably, in the case of some reggae singers who advocate the killing of "batty men" and are never prosecuted). Gayness is no longer classified as a sickness. It is homophobia that is increasingly viewed as the real perversion.

Retreat?

These important advances have, however, coincided with a massive retreat from the ideals and vision of the lesbian and gay liberation pioneers. Most queers no longer question the values, laws and institutions of mainstream society. They happily settle for equal rights with heterosexuals and aspire to little more than a gay version of suburban family life.

Many of us are nowadays carbon copies of heterosexuality. We have internalised straight thinking and become "hetero homos"—straight minds trapped in queer bodies. Our queer psyche has been colonised by a heterosexual mentality. GLF never campaigned for equality. Its demand was gay liberation. We wanted to change society, not conform to it.

How times have changed.

The 1971 GLF Manifesto set out a far-sighted, radical agenda for a non-violent revolution in cultural values and attitudes. It questioned marriage, the nuclear family, monogamy and patriarchy. Making common cause with the women's, blacks' and workers' movements, gay liberationists never sought equality within the status quo. We wanted fundamental social change.

Our idealistic vision involved creating a new sexual democracy, without homophobia, misogyny, racism and class privilege. Erotic shame and guilt would be banished, together with compulsory monogamy, the nuclear family, and rigid male and female gender roles. There would be sexual freedom and human rights for everyone—gay, bi and straight. Our message was "innovate, don't assimilate."

Oh dear. Look what's happened now. Whereas GLF derided the family as "a patriarchal prison that enslaves women, gays and children", the biggest gay campaigns of recent years were for partnership and parenting rights. The focus on these safe, cuddly issues suggests that queers are increasingly reluctant to rock the boat. Many of us would, it seems, prefer to embrace traditional heterosexual aspirations, rather than question them.

This political retreat signifies a huge loss of confidence and optimism. It signals that the lesbian and gay community has finally succumbed—like much of mainstream society—to the depressing politics of conformism, respectability and moderation.[4]

Lesbians in Gay Liberation, London, 1972

Lindsay River gives her views on GLF from a female perspective:

I came out in 1965, went back in, knew I was "really" a lesbian but I was daunted by my mental health struggles at the time. It was not until 1971 when I was at a left wing political conference that I picked up a Gay Liberation Front leaflet from a general bookstall. Reading it, something

---

[4] Our thanks to Peter Tatchell for this fascinating account. For more information about Peter Tatchell's campaigns and to make a donation to them, see his website: **www.petertatchell.net.**

17

very deep shifted in my acceptance of my lesbianism and preparedness to be known as "gay"—in spite of my fear that to do so would inevitably lead to disaster and court the attentions of psychiatry.

Eventually in early 1972, now in a gay relationship, I rang up the GLF number and found out that the women of GLF had just walked out, and were organising separately. We met up and heard that the men did not take on lesbians' issues. I listened, but my girlfriend and I decided we must find out for ourselves. We went to GLF meetings in Brixton where we were the only women, visited the Brixton Faeries in their squats (some Faery might just remember a young woman carrying a kitten in her jacket) and we took on much exciting new information that challenged the whole heterosexual, conventional and capitalist structure of society. Communal living was popular as the alternative to the family. We declared ourselves as non-monogamous, and denounced the police and the psychiatric profession for their oppression of gay people.

We protested with GLF at the second anti-gay "Festival of Light" organised by Mary Whitehouse. We took part in a "Gay In" in Hyde Park, near Speakers' Corner and I remember vividly kissing my girlfriend when we were approached by an Arab man and two women, all in Western clothes. The courteous and obviously sympathetic man explained that his wives did not speak English, but they wanted us to know that they loved each other, just in the same way that we did. There were moving moments of recognition between us, and then in 1970s style we all hugged each other before they walked on.

It was a heady time, flushed with inspiration. My confusion, self questioning and fear about my mental health as a lesbian left me; the pamphlets GLF produced on psychiatry were influential to me.

"After the revolution"

Lindsay River continues:

We saw GLF as part of a wider revolutionary movement, and would fantasise that "after the revolution" (a phrase that tripped off the tongue at that time, not that we ever believed in armed struggle) we should demand the Brighton Pavilion for GLF headquarters! We went to the Bath Alternative Festival to staff the GLF room—where we had the Kinsey scale marked out on cardboard on the floor, running from exclusively gay to exclusively straight and we invited visitors at the festival to stand where they felt they were positioned. They did not all stand at the "only straight" end, by any means. We met some GLF women from Lancaster and started to hitchhike up there, to hang out with the mixed GLF group. We also had a role for women enquirers at the GLF office in Caledonian Road.

We had two dear friends amongst gay men living in Vauxhall, whom I have never been able to reconnect with. We did, however, miss the presence of other women and eventually, by the summer of 1972, we decided to set up a new women-only group at the Vauxhall Women's Centre, called Lesbian Liberation. This is now mainly remembered for its badge which my partner Veronica Dunham[5] designed (it had three women's symbols on it, breaking with the "coupledom" of the double women's symbol).

Around this time a former Gay Lib friend said to me "The gay men don't seem to understand the amount of oppression we experience as women. We have more in common with heterosexual women than with gay men". It was a novel idea to me, coming as I did from having identified as "a female homosexual" in 1965. But by the middle of 1973 I had joined forces with very radical and separatist lesbians, and from that time most of the lesbians I knew organised completely separately from men.

Myself, I am proud to have been a member of GLF in those days, for however short a time. The effect on my thinking, and indeed my personal "liberation", has lasted decades.

GLF Achievements

D Michael Brown gives a further perspective on GLF London:

Looking back from 39 years, my perspective is broader than in my essay of 1978 which was enthusiastic—bubbly and full of the anger and energy which GLF used to have.

Pre-GLF, the approach towards reform of the laws relating to homosexuality had been a moderate one—discussion and lobbying, etc.

---

[5] Veronica (Ronnie) Dunham, a fine artist and musician, died ten years later. She is very much missed.

The Montagu case had generated a great deal of discussion in the late fifties. Much of the excellent work had been done by straight people such as J B Priestley, his wife Jacquetta Hawkes, and Leo Abse MP. One of them lived in the Albany in Piccadilly and that was why they chose the "safe" name "Albany Trust." Gay people themselves had been nervous of getting too involved. If they had come out of their closets there would have been a chance of arrest or of job loss or of exposure through the media.

The pressure on the gay community was building up to a huge extent: the Stonewall riots of June 1969 were the safety valve that released the pressure. That autumn saw the gay community arising and taking their own destiny in their own hands. Disparate groups came together, joined by a rage and desire to overcome their persecutors. There was great urgency and excitement as we felt ourselves making real progress in self improvement, political impact, publicity engendered activities and in finding the keys to our own future. Some of the most noticeable groups with their own agendas within GLF were:

1. Marxists of various types;
2. Left wing trade unions and party workers;
3. Ideological reformers seeking freedom and utopia;
4. An important anarchistic alternative group, rejecting anything hierarchical—one could say a hippy crowd. For a long time it was this group which persuaded GLF that the way forward was an organic response to situations—spontaneity and using those opportunities, reacting to those events as they arose. Power-seekers and ego-trippers were anathema;
5. Members of the older homosexual reform groups;
6. Revolutionaries seeking utopian reform of the whole of society;
7. Feminists and women's libbers and allies who were aware of women's issues in a patriarchal society;
8. Students who were keen on change for better or for worse and who wanted freedom from the Past and from the older generation;
9. A few from the conservative side seeking freedom from the ever darker weight of sexual roles enforced by fear of the law, family exposure and prevailing social morals.

So what were the achievements of GLF? Essentially in my view GLF achieved most of its aims but not immediately. These gains can be seen most clearly in improving attitudes of society which are on-going. I believe it was GLF who largely led to many advances such as discos being set up, a gay press being started, counselling and switchboards—all of which had their roots in GLF. Other things took longer.

Let me give you one concrete example. In January 1971 we held the first GLF Ball at Kensington Town Hall—the very first gay event of its kind in the UK—and the fact that we held it encouraged many other gay groups to hold their functions in a similar open way. It was recorded in the press and photos were taken. As well as reporters there were many police there (apparently they were expecting an orgy). A group carried in a gigantic blow-up penis and the police did nothing about it! Our attitude was that if they arrested one of us then the rest would insist on being arrested too.

It was open to the public and tickets were six old pence (the currency changed later that year). One of the bands playing was, I remember, a black one led by Ginger Johnson. There was dancing and some were smoking joints. But there were no arrests and the next day the *Sunday Express* had photos of it. We had proved a point and helped others to be more open.

South London GLF (c.1972–c.1976)

Trevor Stephens and Marek Levitsky, now members of SLG, reminisce about their days in South London GLF:

GLF South London had a short but exciting history, both socially and politically.

We think the ball was set rolling by adverts in *Private Eye*, because there was no gay paper in those days. Socially we used to meet for our discos in the crypt of St Matthew's Brixton where there was a very supportive and welcoming vicar.

Quite large numbers used to gather there, sometimes up to forty. For licensing reasons we were not allowed to sell alcohol so we used to make our own beer (often made by Marek!) and ask members for a minimum donation of three pence.

St Matthew's Church Brixton where South London GLF first met

I think we always wanted to challenge the other gays and to make them think radically. We wanted to show them that it was possible for gays to be really brave and "in your face" after all the years of repression we had suffered. For this reason many of us dressed up in drag and behaved a bit outrageously! Although I think it's also fair to say that some of us felt the frock brigade were a bit too disruptive, making it even harder for a landlord to accept us when his ordinary customers started to get a bit shocked.

We used to have our socials at the Binfield Hall by Stockwell bus garage. On one occasion we invited a very good steel band, with Trevor both organising and buying the food. It could be frustrating, though, when many of the members were so against capitalism they refused to discuss money and sort out how we were going to pay!

Tony has asked us why we felt the need to dress up in frocks—of course it was not all of us. I think it was to show that gender no longer mattered and there was also the bravery aspect of it—we were just not prepared to be well behaved and silent and closeted—we wanted to tell the whole world that we were "out."

Later we went on to hold discos at a pub in Colliers Wood, used by WAGS prior to us, and also at the White Lion Putney.[6]

The social side was hugely successful with South London GLF, and some life-long friendships and even partnerships were formed.

Railton Road, Brixton

At around the same time there was a squat, I think at 155 Railton Road, Brixton, and we were able to hold serious meetings and discussions there once a week.[7]

---

[6] The White Lion in Putney must be the straight pub in South London to have been used by most gay groups. There is a photo in the Wandsworth-Richmond chapter on Page 71. *Ed.*

[7] There seem to have been several gay squats in Railton Road, some of them next door to each other. *Ed.*

Shying away from controversy

John Brand adds his memories of the GLF Railton Road squat:

I think there was an unbelievably easy-going and ultra-tolerant attitude in the early seventies. I remember I called in one evening at the GLF place in Railton Road and there really was an unusual set of people—some in drag, some hippies preaching gentle revolution, some in motor-bike gear and so on. At some stage in the evening this big tubby guy entered who announced he was into boys, not men, and what could they suggest?

"Oh," said the person on reception cheerfully, "you need to go down to PAL—the Paedophile Action for Liberation. They're in another squat down at the Herne Hill end of Railton Road—in the old barber's shop." After he'd trotted off to the barber's shop, jokes followed about people taking a close shave. But can you imagine anyone nowadays giving friendly advice on that subject, or making a light-hearted joke?

This matched another story about gay journalism of the seventies. *The People* had published a story entitled "The Vilest Men in Britain". Some of their reporters had infiltrated a paedophile discussion group, had photographed them and published the story in their paper together with mug shots.

The next edition of *Gay News* published a retaliatory article entitled, I think, 'The Vilest Reporters in Britain', a kind of spoof of the first article and featuring photos of the intrusive journalists! The attitude of *Gay News* was that everyone had the right to discuss, and we should all stand up for people's basic freedom to do so. ("I disagree with what you say but I will defend to the death your right to say it." *Voltaire*).

But could you picture gay people saying and writing things like that nowadays? Most modern gay campaigners (Peter Tatchell excepted) tend to be politically correct and pro-establishment. They might not go *quite* so far as congratulating *The People* on that article, but they would shy away from doing anything which might offend the powers that be.

Let me give you another example of how things have changed since the seventies.

In the April 2006 issue of *Gay Times* there was something called "Ask Jack" where readers wrote in with their problems. One reader writes to say he has discovered his boyfriend looking at illegal underage pornographic sites on the internet. So here is the (please note) opening sentence of the advice the agony uncle gives him:

"I believe you must speak to the police about your discovery of these child abuse images, however much you love your boyfriend." And he goes on to give the police confidential hotline.

I am offering no opinion about the advice that "Jack" gives, except to say that a reply of that nature in a gay paper would have been *unthinkable* in the days of GLF. Then we were deeply distrustful of the police—now we collaborate with them.

GLF and the Roxy Era

Antony Hardy now gives a musical perspective on GLF:

In my view there was an undoubted link and affiliation between the gay liberation movement in the early seventies and the pop art/music culture of the same period.

The pop world at that time, if you remember, presented itself with its sound, but most especially visually, in a forceful, colourful, unconventional—yet always glamorous and attractive—way. Then pop artists looked as though they were from another (very glam) planet. Yet only ten years previously the Beatles had usually dressed conventionally, in comparison with 1972.

Pop culture of the seventies challenged the straight-based, gender-based attitudes of society and I think they made it easier for GLF etc. to look and to be outrageous and radical. Maybe it helped people to be freer and to be themselves? Groups and artists like Roxy Music (with Brian Ferry and Brian Eno), David Bowie, Lou Reed and Alvin Stardust were inventing their own culture, full of *joie de vivre* and encouraging others to feel the same. Andy Warhol perhaps did something similar in the visual arts.

I would call the music of that era very theatrical, symbolising a glamorous freedom from conventional tastes, as was also GLF. Indeed for young gays it was all a godsend, in my opinion, as it gave us a kind of vehicle through which we could create our own identity and challenge the stereotypes of society.

For me, leaving the army and coming onto the gay scene in the seventies, I found GLF and the current pop music both equally liberating and exciting.[8]

5 Caledonian Road

Now something on a not too roxy address with which GLF was strongly associated. The information is gathered from several sources, including from Albert Beales, who has worked there for many years:

Housmans, at 5 Caledonian Road, is on the left (The trees in the distance are by the side of the Prince Albert/Central Station)

The Housmans bookshop at 5 Caledonian Road, Kings Cross, has an interesting history. Lawrence Housman (brother of the more famous A. E. Housman, the poet) set the bookshop up in 1945 as a centre for left wing

---

[8] Editor's footnote on the word "Roxy": There was a Roxy Cinema near where I lived in Blackheath. It was a very dull area but the cinema had an ornate and stylish décor to it, with brightly coloured pillars and twirly bits—tasteful, yet bold and unconventional. Maybe that was what "roxy" meant?

and peace studies. The idea was to sell any literature which would undermine war and promote justice and freedom.

As early as 1970, GLF leaflets were put on display at Housmans, so it became something of a communications centre. In January 1971 it was decided to establish a GLF office there, in a space at the rear of the basement, rather than just having an accommodation address.

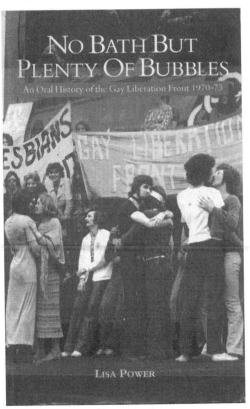

Lisa Power's Book on the History of GLF

Lisa Power continues the story in her fascinating book on GLF, *No Bath But Plenty of Bubbles*: "In 1971 there was a joint Housmans and GLF party in the new office which was disrupted by a group of straight men who, saying they were cadets from Hendon Police College, first tried to gatecrash and then to disrupt the party. They were unceremoniously ejected by the liberationists. A suitable house-warming!"

So from 1971 to 1974 GLF had its office in the basement at 5 Caledonian Road. And with the office being in Housmans, links were created with both anarchist and peace movements. GLF held almost their earliest discos at the Prince Albert (now Central Station) less than 5 minutes walk away, so there was traffic between the two locations.

Prince Albert, Kings Cross (now Central Station)

Albert tells us that about half of the Housmans staff used to go to the Prince Albert; others remember how tolerant and friendly both the staff and the local folk in the downstairs bar used to be!

The disco at the Prince Albert, then a straight local pub, went through most of the seventies—run initially by GLF but later by Gay

Switchboard. So in those days the Switchboard was not just telling people about the gay scene but actually creating it too!

(Robert Liston adds this comment: I just think it's very sad that the self-help ethos has disappeared, to be replaced with a profit-orientated commercial scene).

Unfortunately, by the end of 1973 GLF in London was showing signs of disintegrating. There was particular tension between the more conventional (organisation-minded) members who ran the office at 5 Caledonian Road and the more radical, rather anarchist, members who had set up the "Bethnal Rouge" commune at a bookshop cum warehouse in Bethnal Green. All-London monthly GLF meetings were still being held at the Conway Hall, but these just served to emphasise the disagreements and lead to more arguments, rather than finding common ground.

Events reached their climax in September 1973 when some members of the Bethnal Rouge "raided" the office at Caledonian Road and took away some of the materials there, claiming that they spoke for the true voice of GLF. (*Gay News* reported the incident and added that the South London group was now the only effective GLF group left in London). Feeling themselves almost literally under siege, in February 1974 those still manning the office decided to shut it down—although London Gay Switchboard may well have remained in the upstairs office at 5 Caledonian Road for some time after.

It was sad but perhaps inevitable that, after events like this, middle-of-the-road gays started to become disillusioned with GLF and think about joining or forming other organisations. However, as D Michael Brown said in his part of this chapter: "I believe it was GLF who largely led to many advances such as discos being set up, a gay press being started, counselling and switchboards—all of which had their roots in GLF."

Chapter Three
CHE in London

by Ian Buist and Griff Vaughan Williams

In the West End

Griff begins:

CHEWEG was the name that the London West End group coined for itself. It held its meetings in a public house in St Martin's Lane and then at CHELIC which was CHE's London Information Centre at 22 Great Windmill Street. The Albany Trust was situated not far away in Shaftesbury Avenue.

The building had previously been the headquarters of the National Union of Journalists, and it was Derek Brookfield who had found it for us. He has recently rejoined National CHE.

The CHE London groups were able to have an access programme on London Weekend Television during July 1974. It featured CHE members having a disco on board a boat on the Thames. There was also footage taken at London's Speakers' Corner where CHE activists stood on a step ladder and explained our demands in terms of law and society. It included a sequence with the late Jackie Forster announcing "You're now looking at a roaring lesbian!"

It was during a BBC Radio London broadcast that listeners found out that a London base had been established—there were reps from several London CHE groups taking part. Martin George (who ran the special interest collective, the Motoring Group) acted as manager of CHELIC, transforming the basement into a welcoming centre of activity.

Some members of the national executive committee were quite envious of London CHE being able to support its own headquarters and did not always approve of it.

Another very important event was CHE putting on its own revue *Hello, Mother! Hello, Father!* at the Mercury Theatre in 1974.

CHE Players present
the new gay comedy sensation

HELLO, MOTHER!
HELLO, FATHER!

by BUTCH BLACK

directed by KEN HOLLAND

MERCURY THEATRE

2 LADBROKE ROAD, W.11   LICENSED BAR

Jan., Thurs. 17th - Wed. 23rd, at 8 p.m.

ADMISSION: 70p   NOT SUITABLE FOR CHILDREN

"Very, very Funny"   "Banned"

"Hilarious"   "Riotous"   "Must be seen!"

TEAR HERE   POST TODAY!

To: HELLO, MOTHER! HELLO, FATHER!
CHE-LIC, 22 Gt. Windmill Street, London W.1

Please send me............seats at 70p for the performance

on .... or .... (give alternative).

I enclose a P.O./Cheque No.......................... crossed and
payable to "Hello, Mother! Hello, Father!" and a stamped
addressed envelope, for the return of my tickets.

NAME...

ADDRESS..

THE FLORENTINA PRESS LTD. (T.U.)   3 BIRKBECK HILL, LONDON, S.E.21   01-670 5206

The editor adds:

Probably inspired by CHE's example, in 1975 *Homosexual Acts* was put on
at the Almost Free Theatre, the first completely "out" gay revue in the
West End. Audiences flocked to see it and they all seemed to be very
accepting of the main themes of gay liberation.

Back to Griff:

One amusing aspect of CHELIC at 22 Great Windmill Street was that their phone number by chance had only one digit different from that of the London Palladium. This meant that people phoning up to book tickets for Larry Grayson's performance at the Palladium sometimes misdialled and were answered by "This is the Campaign for Homosexual Equality."

22 Great Windmill Street, now an Internet café

Concern for the older gay

One of the West End Group's most important other activities was a publication on the needs of the aged gay man and lesbian. Some 500 copies were sold around the world, with the university at Ann Arbour in Michigan ordering numerous copies. In the meantime a group called the August

Trust was formed to establish accommodation for elderly gays and lesbians. In turn the September group was formed to be a social group for them.

The organisation Age Concern also changed its attitude and became more sympathetic after they had seen the report.

Some notable names

Allan Horsfall was involved with CHE from the start, ever since CHE was launched as the Committee for Homosexual Equality. In fact it was his association with the Albany Trust's Homosexual Law Reform Society, and his desire to be an activist on the issue in the North West, that led to CHE being formed. It was not long before he was made CHE's Life President. These days he is kept busy—along with CHE Vice-President Ray Gosling—in keeping an eye on cases in courts, with their Gay Monitor project.

We were sad to hear that Alan Louis, who had been on the CHE Executive for a decade, passed away while this book was being written. He had been convenor of the former local London group covering the Kilburn area. It was Alan who in about 2005 brought to the surface the whole issue of "murder music" lyrics. His main interest in later years had been older gays and their housing needs.

Ian Buist continues:

The right approach

On 8 May 1972 I trod gingerly up the steps into Fulham Town Hall, where I had learnt that a new organisation, the Campaign for Homosexual Equality, was holding a dance. I found myself among people looking reassuringly ordinary, many from the same middle class background from which I myself came. (It was a revelation to see how matter-of-fact the Town Hall staff were at this invasion!). I arranged forthwith to join, and was assigned to "Group 13", then led by Richard Nicholas.

I was convinced that CHE had the right approach towards the huge task of changing public opinion, following the opening made by the 1967 Act and the subsequent much-publicised events following the "Stonewall riots". I did not think that the Gay Liberation Front, which saw the need as being to destroy all relevant social structures, had the right message, although their key principle—that we have to accept ourselves first before we can ask others to accept us—was a fundamental truth.

Fulham Town Hall, then used for dances by both GLF and CHE

Within a short time I was invited to an "induction meeting" held at Roger Baker's flat, in which we were introduced more thoroughly to the workings and aims of CHE. I noticed one older man positively trembling with fear and emotion at this discussion—probably the first time he had revealed his own orientation to anyone at all, let alone met others who were gay. I gave him a lift back to Hammersmith Broadway to catch his Tube to Ealing or Wembley. He could not stop talking, so we went round and round until at last I pulled in to the side and waited until he felt able to take his leave.

Some weeks later I got a letter from him which bubbled over with his sense that he was at last able to be himself, in touch with others of the same kind; they were starting a local group; he was helping to organise a large social programme—in short, his real life had at last begun. From that moment I realised just what CHE could do, and was determined to help as far as I was able.

I myself had revealed my sexuality to my Civil Service masters two years earlier, upon being "positively vetted" for security following my return from Africa. I survived that ordeal thanks entirely to the cool and enlightened attitude of my Permanent Secretary, Sir Geoffrey Wilson, who sanctioned my clearance against the advice of the Security Service and despite the misgivings of other Permanent Secretaries.

National CHE Conferences

After gaining recognition we were given the chance, as individual members, to take part in CHE's first National Conference at Morecambe (April 1973). This was attended by some 300 people, and was dominated by arguments on future policy: should we be campaigning solely for equality under the existing legal framework, or should we be seeking to have it radically rethought, especially in relation to sexual activity by those under the age of consent? Our Wandsworth-Richmond committee had discussed this and we weighed in strongly in favour of the former. But no conclusions were reached, and the issue came up again at the 1974 Conference, held at Malvern. This had a very different "feel" to it; there was a civic reception, people in Malvern were very friendly, and some 800 members attended, together with representatives from the Scottish Minorities Group (SMG).

It was decided to take the whole matter in two stages. It was urgent to equalise the existing law, and work on detailed proposals for this were to begin at once. In the longer term, there should also be research and other work on whether a whole new approach was needed in all sexual offences legislation. This allowed Ike Cowen, CHE's Legal Adviser and an Executive member, to launch detailed drafting work on a reforming law. Malvern was also notable for being the occasion at which Sir Angus Wilson, the writer, 'came out' about his 25-year relationship—a statement which guaranteed wide (if not always helpful) publicity.

In 1975 the Conference was at Sheffield, and a huge and unwieldy number—over 2,000—attended. For the first time there was a substantial cohort of women, who made very clear their feelings about the preponderance of "male issues" in CHE's work, but perhaps were less clear on how to remedy this.

In 1976 the Conference took place at Southampton but I could not attend. (In fact I only managed thereafter to go to the meetings at York in 1980 and, in 1981, in Durham—a landmark for me since it was there that I met my life-partner. I now attend the small annual Conferences in London).

Changing the Law

CHE concluded preparation of its draft Sexual Offences (Amendment) Bill in 1975 and published it widely among MPs. (I wrote to Hugh Jenkins, then a junior Minister and MP for Putney, to seek his support.) The Government reacted by sending the whole issue the next year to the Criminal Law Revision Committee and its Policy Advisory Group. CHE put together a very substantial submission to the Commission, which included the Bill but also much other relevant material.

When this finally reported in 1978, it recommended changing the age of consent to 18 but did not grant the principle of equality thereby or in other ways. CHE had made extensive and very thorough submissions to the Committee and we were disappointed by the outcome. But the solid work already done enabled us locally to lobby many MPs.

The Thatcher years

With the advent of the Thatcher Governments, and throughout the '80s, the hopes of any significant legal change shrank to nearly nil and indeed even the recommendations of the CLRC were ignored. Instead, attention focussed first on the advent of AIDS and its implications for the gay community and then on what became the obnoxious "Section 28"—not repealed until 2003. But occasional discussion over the age of consent (a touchstone) continued, and there was a gradual shift towards our point of view in successive votes in Parliament, as society became more open.

The re-emergence of campaigning with the emergence of Stonewall greatly intensified the pressure for change. It was gratifying that Putney's own MP, David Mellor, finally came round to supporting an age of consent of 16. Nevertheless it is a commentary on the British political system that only in 2002–03 was the principle of equal treatment in the criminal law accepted by the Government. Even these changes would not have been made without continued pressure and a series of judgments by the European Court of Human Rights. (Ironically, it was Mrs Thatcher who paved the way for this by deciding to continue the right of individual appeal to the Court—to allow dissidents to challenge striking trade unions).

It was on 3 May 1979, on the same day as the long reign of Margaret Thatcher began, that I achieved one of my own proudest ambitions. I succeeded in getting the "Mandarins' Union", the FDA (First Division Association), to accept at its Annual Conference a motion adopting a policy of equality for homosexual people in the Service, against the tacit obstruction of the Executive platform. To its honour the FDA has stuck rigidly to this ever since. I had to deploy many of the manoeuvres I had witnessed at CHE's Annual Conferences.

CHE Changes Itself

At its 1980 York Conference CHE had decided to separate its campaigning and social fund-raising efforts, starting something called "CHE Enterprises". I did not myself think this wise, and I believe that it was proved a mistake by subsequent events, as it led to a steady decline in CHE's own central funding and hence its ability to function effectively.

CHE is now a pale shadow of its former glory, but it has real achievements of which to boast, and it succeeded in making the whole cause of equality "respectable" by its professional efforts during the 1970s. More important, it provided a welcome home and meeting-place for those who had never before thought that they could have their own lives—much less work for, and hope to see, better days.

Editor's note:

Our thanks to Griff and to Ian for their accounts of CHE in London. There is of course much more about the CHE local London groups in several later chapters.

Chapter Four
London Monday Group 1971–

by Bob Cook, Richard Miles and Brian Parker

Formerly the London Monday Group for Homosexual Equality, LMG, (as it is now known) is one of the two or three longest surviving gay groups in the country. The London Monday Group never had any connections with the Tory Monday Club, and got its name because it met on a Monday. It was briefly renamed "The West London Group" but as you read through its history you will see why this was not too accurate a title!

The Chepstow Arms, Notting Hill

LMG began as CHE London Group Ten but linked, in its earliest days, with Bloomsbury Group, Group Four. Howarth Penny was one notable person, being the paid general secretary of CHE and also a member of LMG. The first meetings were at a church in Broadley Terrace or at John Saxby's flat in South Kensington. Later we moved to the Two Brewers in Monmouth Street and then to the Thebes Restaurant in Bell Street, NW1. Then for many years LMG met at the Chepstow Arms.

There was one eighteen month break from the Chepstow as far as meetings were concerned, when the pub was being renovated, and proceedings were switched to the hall of St Stephen's, a very Gothic church in Royal Oak.

The Champion, Notting Hill Gate

In 1971 our first convenor and secretary were John Saxby and Angus Easson, respectively, with St John Adlard, of whom more below, becoming speakers' secretary in 1978. From 1982 we were no longer a CHE group as CHE had dissolved its national network—the convenor was Philip Weston and the secretary Rob Walker, with St John continuing as speakers' secretary. In 1985 Bob Cook and Brian Parker joined the committee for the first time. In 2000 Bob Cook, Ron Hastings, Brian Parker and Chris Reilly took over as trustees. Bob sadly died in 2009, but the others have been involved ever since.

The Champion, not far from the Chepstow, was then a gay pub and we would hold informal pub evenings there.

Back to St John's achievements:

St John Adlard had huge success in persuading celebrities to come along. Speakers included Leo Abse (the wonderful and brave Labour MP mainly responsible for getting the law against homosexuality repealed, and who has only recently passed away), Bernard Miles, Sue Pollard, Maria Aitken, Rabbi Julia Neuberger, Lord Longford twice and Lord Soper twice, not to mention countless MPs, councillors and clergymen.

On Kenneth Williams' first visit to us, some members attacked him for not being sufficiently "out"—this was in 1977. *The Kenneth Williams Diaries*, edited by Russell Davies (Harper Collins 1993) states:

> 1st June 1977—The letters include one from CHE, the homosexual group for equality, asking me to talk to them! Heaven knows what about! *(p 542)*

> 27th June 1977—Michael came to drive me to the Chepstow for this talk to CHE. The room was packed.
>
> There was a lot of sniping from a journalist, called Robert something, about stereotyping "limp queens" and giving the public an erroneous image etc, etc, and a dreadful man who got very emotional and said "It's people like you that get queers spat at."
>
> I said "People spat on Oscar Wilde before I was born" whereupon his friend cried out "Why don't you give us your support at the Old Bailey where *Gay News* is being prosecuted by Mary Whitehouse?"
>
> I said I needed notice of that question—I know nothing about this case. (A Professor Kirkup has written a homosexual poem about a centurion and Christ. It sounds banal and pathetic.) *(p 545)*

The next time Kenneth Williams came to speak—yes, it was remarkable he came back wasn't it?—he told us about his friendship with Joe Orton and Kenneth Halliwell.

He had been on holiday with them in Tangier just weeks before their tragic deaths in London. Apparently the couple had fewer quarrels when a sympathetic third person, like Williams, was with them.

Orton (left) with Williams and Halliwell,
Windmill Café, Tangier Beach, 1967

Lord Longford addressed the group on 5 June 1978 on the subject of Christianity and Morality. A letter to the editor of *The Guardian* on 1 December 1995 from Henry D Robertson stated: "Your profile of Lord Longford recalled to mind a meeting of the Campaign for Homosexual Equality, at which he was a guest speaker. He assured us all that, although Christ was nowhere recorded as having condemned 'homosexualism', He would have done so had He been asked. When I expressed surprise that Lord Longford felt competent to speak on behalf of the Son of God, he went into a paroxysm of rage and accused *me* of being arrogant."

Lord Longford is remembered by us as being very tall and rather surprising us by his choice of drinks (complimentary, please note!)—sherry, beers, gin & tonic, amongst other incongruous beverages.

In 1978 Dr Charlotte Bach addressed a meeting of LMG, at which the late Bill Barron, looking at the tall, heavily featured central European speaker, was heard to whisper "That's not a woman, that's a man in drag!" Following her death in 1981, it transpired that she was in fact a man, born Carl Hajdu in 1920, the son of a Hungarian baron, and this came as a great surprise to some of her devotees. The story rather implies that the biographer was present at the meeting. Dr Bach explained to LMG her theories on human ethology, showing that diversity of sexuality had been a driving force of evolution.

St John recalls that after an invitation was sent to Billy Connolly he received a phone call in which it became clear that Billy believed it to be a hoax, doubting anyone could really be called St John Adlard and assuming that Kenny Everett was playing a joke on him. Having spoken to St John, he realised his mistake and agreed to come! He presented St John with a home-made quiche and gave a witty but thought-provoking talk which was one of the all-time highspots of the group's speakers' programme.

Other celebrities included Alan Hollinghurst, author of the very successful gay novel, *The Swimming Pool Library*, Maureen Duffy and Henry Kelly. With speakers of this calibre it was hardly surprising that numbers at meetings were very high, with an average of around 30 even when the speaker was not so well known! Even some of the members of LMG itself in those days were quite illustrious, such as Denis Lemon, the editor of *Gay News*, and Michael Mason.

At about the same time we tried out a new policy of inviting along guest speakers who were not particularly sympathetic. One of these was the playwright John Osborne, and his refusal prompted some lively correspondence in the *Evening Standard*, some of which we quote below. (Needless to say it can only have done the group good so far as publicity was concerned!). A journalist writing for the *Standard*'s Londoner's Diary wrote, under the heading "Shout Back in Anger":

"A case of eternal optimism you might think. Ignoring Osborne's notorious queer-bashing outbursts—or I suppose ignorant of them—the West London Group for Homosexual Equality asked the famous playwright to speak. Came back Osborne's reply, borrowing Oscar's phrase in cruel form: 'I have little sympathy for such a movement and feel that the love which dares not speak its name should settle down a bit.' "

A few days later they published our reply to the above: "We have over ten years had several hundred guest speakers and we can assure everyone we did not contact John Osborne out of ignorance as has been suggested. No guest of ours would have had a 'bitchy' reception (as another correspondent had suggested)." (St John Adlard).

Shout back in anger

A CASE of eternal optimism, you might think. Ignoring John Osborne's notorious queer-bashing outbursts — or, I suppose, ignorant of them — the West London Group for Homosexual Equality asked the famous playwright to speak.

Came back Osborne's reply, borrowing Oscar's phrase in cruel form: "I have little sympathy for such a movement and feel that the love that dare not speak its name should settle down a bit."

This splenetic missive was received calmly by the Group's St John Adelard. "Quite frankly," he replied to Osborne, "you would have been an ideal person to come along to talk on it does make such a refreshing change."

The *Evening Standard* reports on John Osborne's
refusal to speak to the London Monday Group

Shortly after the above correspondence, *Capital Gay* reported (18 July 1986) that a London-wide quiz was to be started by LMG. This was of course the beginning of the annual Capital Quiz. We are putting in a list of the dates when a group has won just for its first time, because it gives a fascinating picture of the diversity of the gay groups in London:

1987	London L & G Switchboard	1988	Haringey Gay Group
1989	Hampstead Area Gay Soc	1990	Jungle Reds
1991	*Gay Times*	1993	DELGA
1994	Gay Football Supporters	1997	Pink Angels
1998	London Monday Group	2001	NW1
2002	Bugle Boys	2003	Central Station, Kings Cross
2006	Black Cap, Camden Town.		

Just for the record DELGA (Lib Dems for L & G Action) is the only group to have won more than twice—they have in fact won it four times!

The first event in the series of quizzes was held on 27 November 1986 at the Chepstow and it has always been associated with our group. In the early days it changed its venue for each round. Then every round was held at the Locomotive in Camden Town for a while, then either at Central Station or, more often, at the Black Cap, Camden Town.

The Black Cap, Camden Town, where the Capital Quiz was often held

Back to the London Monday Group itself

Unfortunately there were difficulties at our meetings at the Chepstow with a rather hostile landlady, and we were told to go. First of all we went to the Apple Tree in Mount Pleasant, so for the first time we were away from West London, where Duncan Campbell, the radical well-known journalist, spoke to us.

From there we went to the Mortimer Arms in Tottenham Court Road. Not our best venue! The barman there used to shout out when a speaker was on, asking "Would any of you people be wanting a little drink?" He did this once when Michael Palin was our guest speaker. Luckily he could see the funny side!

Soon after this we moved to the Locomotive in Camden Town: speakers at the Locomotive included Richard O'Brien of the *Rocky Horror Show*, who arrived with a female partner driving a pink Rolls Royce, Glenda Jackson (who was standing as MP for Hampstead), George Melly and Gordon Kay of *'Allo 'Allo*, the late George Schlesinger, the pianist Peter Katin and novelist Francis King.

In 2008 Central Station had to temporarily close down and we moved to Penderel's Oak, the Wetherspoons pub in High Holborn. Although Central Station has re-opened we have decided to convene at Penderel's Oak every Monday at 8 pm.

We arrange two short breaks abroad every year for members, the first in May and the second in August. We are represented on two councils of voluntary services, and we meet up frequently with other groups under the SLAGO umbrella.

We welcome new members who can get in touch with us through the SLAGO website.

Editor's note:

Sadly Bob Cook passed away only a short while after giving us his notes on the group, and he will be much missed. We are very glad we were able to include all the valuable memories of LMG he gave us.

Chapter Five
The Marypad Group 1971–

by Malcolm Malins and Rodney Wilson

Early Days

In the 1970s CHE was constructing local groups as soon as it had enough people in each area to form one. Our founder, Ken Glazier, who was a member of CHE London Group 2, was delegated to form Group 6, which adopted the name Marylebone and Paddington Group.

The first meeting was on 19th May 1971 in the Coach & Horses just off Oxford Street. After a few meetings the group moved to the Alliance Hall in Westminster, then the Victoria Arms at Victoria;. then for much longer periods at the Royal Scottish, Fetter Lane; a church hall near Marylebone Station; briefly at CHE's headquarters in Great Windmill Street; then for a long time at the Coachmakers' Arms in Marylebone Lane; and for a while at the Community Centre, Westbourne Grove.

The Coachmakers' Arms, Marylebone Lane

These venues were for public meetings which were advertised in the gay press and were open for anyone to come along to meet others and hopefully join the Group. There were some high profile speakers at these meetings, including Donald Soper, Rabbi Lionel Blue, Angus Wilson, Quentin Crisp, and local MPs. On other occasions there were spokesmen from the local police, the Albany Trust, transvestite and transsexual societies, as well as various luminaries from CHE including Allan Horsfall, Jackie Forster and Babs Todd. The founders of Gay's the Word bookshop came along, as did also a spokesman for the Gay Wrestlers, but the leading gay travel company of the time declined our invitation.

Meetings with speakers were often held jointly with other groups which usually ensured a good attendance in the earlier days, but due to falling attendance at these public meetings they were discontinued several years ago.

The group was active on the campaigning front in the early years and attended the annual CHE conferences at Morecambe, Malvern, Sheffield, Southampton, Nottingham and York, and the Gayfest event at Durham University. The Group also took part in the Gay Pride marches in London carrying the Group's own banner and was a major participant in the first CHE Winter Fair in London.

Social Occasions

In addition to the monthly public meetings the Group has always had a strong social element: it has met and still does meet weekly in members' homes, usually on Tuesdays, for either a coffee or drinks evening or sometimes a meal out in a restaurant.

There have always been visits to galleries and to concerts, like the Wallace Collection or lakeside at Kenwood, and a few stranger places such as the London Dungeon and the Zoo, with bonfire and fireworks parties in November and summer garden parties at the homes of members living a little out of town. There is an annual birthday party and another at Christmas, and in the past on New Year's Eve too—with a game of Charades to pass the time away towards midnight. The 25th anniversary of the group was celebrated at the Conway Hall in 1996 with members past and present attending.

There were film shows featuring hired 16 mm copies of current box office hits and early on a couple of "other" film shows. How on earth did we get our hands on copies of *Boys in the Sand* and *Bijou* back in the 1970s?—you couldn't just go into Prowler or Clonezone, which didn't exist then, and pick them off the shelves. There was a hired stripper at one party—enough said ... what decadence!

The social outings have extended further afield with trips abroad about once a year. Members have arranged weekend (and longer) visits to Paris, Lisbon, Copenhagen, Brussels, Vienna, Berlin and Amsterdam. There was one occasion, in 1990, when eight members in two groups were touring California at the same time. Paths crossed when in San Francisco. The Amsterdam trips have continued on an annual basis until just a few years ago. Some members went for the tourist sites, some for the trams, some to enjoy the opera and culture, some to enjoy, well, shall we say, the night life (more decadence).

The membership at its peak was about 50, which even included members in Brussels, Andorra, Australia and New Zealand. It is possible, but not confirmed from records or memories, that the gay serial killer Dennis Neilson became a member. Apparently when searching his flat the police found a copy of our newsletter which suggested he might have been. However, no members of the group were found to have "gone missing" during this period!

Today, due to the passage of time many members from those early days are no longer with us, and with the wide range of gay social activities available in London and elsewhere the membership is now down to 20, only one of whom was there at the beginning. The Group still raises funds through an annual subscription and a collection, currently £1, at each meeting. Our stall at the Winter Fair also used to raise a substantial sum. The funds raised are given to gay causes, which have included CHE, Terrence Higgins Trust/Lighthouse, Gay Switchboard and London Friend.

If anyone would like to get in touch with us we would be very pleased to hear from you. E-mail us at **malcolm.rm@ntlworld.com**.

Chapter Six
The Croydon Group 1971–

by Ross Burgess

Beginnings

In early 1971 Andy V went to a packed CHE group meeting in Holborn: one of several London CHE groups that had recently started up. He got talking to some other people about the lack of facilities for gay people in Croydon, and this led him to start weekly meetings in his big flat on South Norwood Hill.

After a few months Andy decided to move on to other things, and the group was put on a new footing, as an official CHE group. London CHE groups at that time were given numbers, so the Croydon group became London Group Seven. New members joining CHE were sometimes allocated to Group Seven irrespective of where they lived!

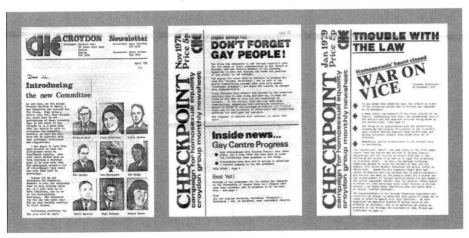

However Group Seven was rather different from the other London groups, having a particular geographical focus, and a catchment area that extended far beyond London. By 1972 the group had renamed itself "CHE Croydon" or "Croydon CHE Group", and the next year it opted out of the London Convenors Collective.

The group held monthly meetings at the Cherry Orchard, in Cherry Orchard Road, but in January 1972 members arriving at the pub were told they were no longer welcome. The meetings then moved to the Unitarian Church Hall on Croydon Flyover, where they continued on and off for years. Early speakers included the Bishop of Croydon, who nominated one of his clergy to be a link with the group, and Quentin Crisp. There were also seminars aimed at teachers, doctors, the police, and the general public.

Alongside the formal meetings there have always been events in members' homes: coffee evenings, wine and cheese, and video evenings, plus parties for Christmas/New Year, Halloween, St Valentine's Day, and any other opportunity. Amongst the earliest members to host events were Rose Robertson, who went on to found a group for the parents of gay children, and the distinguished pianist Peter Katin (still a Vice-President of CHE) who held fundraising concerts in his house.

Group Seven's first convenor (although he generally referred to himself as "Chairman") was Wallace Grevatt, who later became known as an expert on BBC Radio and author of a book on *Radio Times*. Wallace stood down after a year, but later became active in national CHE.

After a year or so, the Croydon group was getting quite big, and covering a wide geographical area, so it was decided to institute a regional structure. Wallace Grevatt, who was now the CHE national executive member looking after local groups, advised against this (the official solution being to set up new groups if one group got too big) but his advice was rejected. Individual Committee members now looked after particular areas, such as Central Croydon, Streatham, Upper Norwood, Bromley, and Redhill. This lasted until 1980, when it was abandoned because fewer people were coming forward to join the Committee (and separate groups had meanwhile been set up in some of these areas).

During the early years there was a lot of interaction with national CHE: Croydon members attended the annual Conferences and the quarterly National Councils, and on occasion helped to host a National Council in London. In July 1977 the entire Committee, plus about 30 members and friends, took part in the Gay Pride March in London.

In 1978 Peter Wells joined the group, and became a very active and outspoken member. He had been given 2½ years in jail for having sex with two 18-year-olds, and was suing the British Government as a result. The next year he was murdered in an unrelated incident, and the CAGS Tennis Group later named a trophy in his honour.

The Star Discos and the Gay Centre Fund

Nigel Webb took over as Chairman in 1976 and the change was immediately evident in the Newsletters, which frequently featured Nigel's editorial comments. From the outset he laid great stress on the "Three Cs"—Campaigning, Caring, and Companionship. One of the campaigns during this time was a dispute with Croydon Library, which had banned *Gay News*. The group organised demonstrations and a "read-in" (members would bring their own copies to read in the library and then leave them behind for others to read) and the ban was eventually overturned.

The group also started discussions with Croydon Police about the large numbers of arrests for cottaging, particularly in "Kathy's" (the public toilet next to the police station). Kathy's has long since been replaced with modern superloos, and the police station itself has been demolished: the site is now part of the Queen's Gardens.

Nigel's leadership came at times under criticism, for instance his evident left-wing leanings were sometimes thought to conflict with CHE's policy of avoiding party politics. But he certainly helped to invigorate the group.

At this time the commercial gay disco scene had not got started, and many local groups decided to run their own discos. Discos were started at several venues in Croydon and South London, but by far the most successful were those that the group organised at the Star in London Road, Broad Green (now the Broad Green Tavern) mainly on a Saturday evening.

The Stargaze discos (as they were later called) were a very important source of funds to the group, although requiring quite a bit of commitment from committee members and others to be there and collect the money. The principal DJ at the Star was Croydon's own Colin Peters, who started his career there before going on to greater things in central London. At times there were as many as 240 people at the Star, not all of whom would be group members. However members did benefit for a time from cheaper admission, and the membership numbers reached an all-time high of 180.

From time to time there had been suggestions that Croydon should have its own Gay Centre, and the large amounts of money coming in from the Star discos made this idea seem not unrealistic. The group even got as far as considering a couple of possible premises, but one would have required too much work to put it right and another was dropped because of difficulties in raising a loan. Then competition in the form of a commercial gay disco at the Greyhound reduced the takings from the Star (the Star discos were abandoned in 1982) and the prospect of a Gay Centre began to seem less attainable. Enthusiasm began to wane, and at one point there was a move to suspend the group's activities altogether.

From CHE to CAGS

From 1981 onwards, national CHE had been debating major changes in its structure. It had long been combining two roles: a national campaigning body, and a network of local groups. Some people on the National Executive felt that it would be better to split the two roles, and hive off the local groups to a new Gay Community Organisation (GCO). The Croydon CHE committee were sceptical about this arrangement (and with hindsight it's pretty obvious that the split was damaging to both the social and the campaigning aspects of CHE's work) but it went ahead anyway. The Croydon Group declined to join GCO, or to use the Gay Centre Fund to buy shares in it (and by 1984 GCO had been wound up anyway).

A special general meeting was held in October 1982 to put the Croydon group on a new footing, with a new name. Following the example of WAGS, GAGS (Guildford) and KRAGS, the obvious name was Croydon Area Gay Society (CAGS) but the meeting decided in favour of CALGS (Croydon Area Lesbian and Gay Society). The meeting also considered the future of the Gay Centre Fund: recognising that the dream of a Croydon Gay Centre had evaporated, it was decided to make some immediate grants, and keep the bulk of the money earning interest to fund gay causes. Later the fund was put in the care of trustees and afterwards renamed "the Special Fund".

The group's new name was controversial: some members maintained that the L was unnecessary since the word "gay" can apply to both sexes. When Clive Morgan became Chair in 1984 he decided to ignore the official name, and promote the group as CGS (Croydon Gay Society). At the following AGM this was proposed as the official name, but the meeting chose CAGS instead, which it has remained ever since.

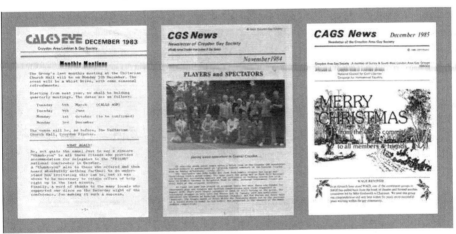

The group right from its outset has struggled to recruit women members, despite putting on events aimed particularly at women from time to time. We had one female chair (Jane Fuller) but only for a year, and in the year or so that followed there was little to appeal to lesbians: the Newsletter regularly featured a "Page 3 Hunk", and regular trips were organised to male-oriented gay beaches such as Telscombe Cliffs.

From 1981 the group was a member of SAGO (later SLAGO—the Surrey and London Association of Gay Organisations).

AIDS and the ACE Project

In June 1984 the Newsletter reported that a vaccine for AIDS was expected within two to five years, and that the first local AIDS victim was in Mayday Hospital. By 1988 there was an urgent need to provide local services for people with AIDS, and CAGS got together with other local organisations to set up what became the ACE Project (AIDS Care Education). Once again CAGS had a new purpose and a cause to raise money for, and the ACE Follies in 1989 and 1990 were particularly memorable, as well as raising substantial sums for the project.

The January 1990 Newsletter had photos of Mike Harvey and Ray Amer, two CAGS members who had been particularly active in the project, at the opening of the ACE Centre at Queens Hospital. Sadly the very next Newsletter had a report of Mike's death, but Ray (now Ray Harvey-Amer) is still very active on behalf of CAGS 20 years later.

Quite a few CAGS events were held at the ACE Centre, which later moved to premises in Mitcham, but by 2001 changes in NHS funding, and the development of more effective ways of treating AIDS, meant that it was no longer viable, and it finally closed in 2003.

CAGS in the 1990s

Reg Jones took over as Chair of the group in 1989, and held this office on and off for several years. During this time the main focus of the group (alongside ongoing involvement in the ACE Project) was on social events. In 1992 there were film shows every week, hosted by Tony Everett, who had been Chair of CAGS several years before.

From 1991 onwards CAGS was represented on the CCPCC (now the CCPCG—Croydon Community Police Consultation Group). Relations with Croydon Council had also much improved. LGBT-related items were included in the new Croydon Museum, and in 1993 six members of CAGS presented the Mayor of Croydon with 20 pink carnations, each representing a thousand gay people in Croydon.

Croydon Pride was celebrated in June 1993 with a full programme of events at the Bird in Hand, the Hollybush (Crystal Palace), PJs (Thornton Heath) and Streets Bar (Penge), plus buses to take people to the Pride Parade in central London and then on to the Pride Festival in Brockwell Park. The Croydon Pride brochure listed seven participating groups[9]. The following year however Croydon Pride was dissolved through lack of support, but the CAGS banner continued to be carried in the Pride Parade.

In 1994 a social sub-committee was set up to organise the group's social events, but four years later they stood down, saying that they'd organised some good events, but often only sub-committee members themselves had turned up. In 1995 David Page (Secretary since 1990) became Chair of CAGS, a position he still holds in 2010, making him by far the longest-serving Chair in the group's history.

In 1997 the Croydon Lesbian and Gay Forum (later the Croydon LGBT Forum) was founded with the aim of representing all LGBT people in Croydon. It held regular meetings, and organised a series of cultural events in the Braithwaite Hall.

---

[9] Croydon Pride Organising Group, CAGS, CAGY, Croydon Friend, the Croydon Lesbian and Gay Monitor, the Croydon Lesbian Social Support Group, the Sisters of Perpetual Indulgence.

Tennis and other special interests

The Tennis Group has been a feature of the group's life since about 1977. For most of that time they have played tennis every Sunday, first at Park Hill and latterly at Thornton Heath, with finals days twice a year. Some of the current players have been competing for over 30 years. For some years there was also tennis on a Wednesday evening in the summer and badminton in the winter.

In 1974 the Newsletter reported various special interest groups being set up, including jazz, bridge, photography, and transport. By "transport" it clearly meant the Transport Group, but this seems to be a mistake: several of the Transport Group's leading members came from Croydon, but it was never actually part of Croydon CHE. The 1997 AGM decided to set up a Special Interests Network ("SIN list") for any member who wished to advertise their interests and phone numbers (later also e-mail addresses).

Croydon Friend

In 1973 a Croydon branch of Friend, the counselling and befriending organisation, was set up. Its main purpose was to support isolated people and help launch them into gay society or address their gay-related problems. About ten people a week on average responded to Friend's adverts in the local paper. Trans people and married partners were referred to the relevant groups. Friend continued for many years, at one time offering a drop-in facility as well as the help line, and was supported by social events including Geoff Galpin's well-remembered Sunday tea parties.

The Youth Group

Croydon Area Gay Youth (CAGY) was very successful in the late 1980s and at one time had more members than CAGS. Relations with CAGS were sometimes strained, for instance when CAGY raised its cut-off age to 30 and was accused of competing with CAGS for members. But for long periods CAGY events were advertised in the CAGS Newsletter and all CAGS events were open to CAGY members. The two groups came closest together in 1982 when Roy Nixon was simultaneously Chair of both. Eventually CAGY came to an end, probably owing to a lack of new people to help run it. Since then a number of youth groups have come and gone under various names, all run for young people by public bodies rather than run by young people themselves.

A Variety of Venues

Several church premises have been used by the group over the years. The Unitarian Church Hall has already been mentioned, and we also had meetings for a while at Croydon Parish Church Hall.

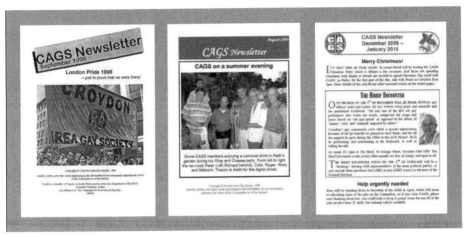

St John the Evangelist Upper Norwood was associated with the group for many years: we booked the church hall regularly on a Wednesday evening, often for badminton in the main hall and social get-togethers for CAGS and/or CAGY in the lounge. The church itself held special services for World AIDS Day during the ACE period. In 2004 we re-enacted the ceremonies that ancient churches had used to join people of the same sex, and asked about using St John's hall for this, but the then vicar, David Martin, insisted we should use the church itself.

We have also had regular meetings in various pubs around the borough. We used the Croydon at the corner of Park Street and St George's Walk from 1973 until we were banned in 1985, and then again from 1991, but it's now long since been boarded up. The Goose and Carrot (formerly the Horse and Jockey) was a favourite venue for a while, and we used its cellar for memorable SLAGO quizzes. In 1987 we heard that the

Bird in Hand was becoming gay, and we've had events there from time to time ever since (it was briefly renamed the Bird of Pride).

Other pubs mentioned in the Newsletters have included the Duke of Clarence, the Sun, the Gun, PJs (Bar 68), the Oval Tavern, the Wheelwrights, the Oakfield, the Hollybush, the Swan and Sugarloaf, the Whistle Stop, and the Greyhound.

The New Millennium

Croydon in the 21ˢᵗ Century has seen the disappearance of the remaining gay venues, except for the Bird in Hand: there's a tower block going up on the site of the Goose and Carrot, and even the Southern Pride in West Norwood has gone straight and changed its name.

Croydon Friend finally closed in 2001. An LGBT policing forum (Aurora) has been set up, and the Croydon LGBT Forum has been disbanded (bequeathing some of its members to CAGS) and subsequently replaced by Crocus (Croydon's LGBT Network).

In 2009 and 2010 Croydon Council supported LGBT History Month, with an exhibition and reception in the Croydon Clocktower. In 2010 the Deputy Mayor opened the expanded LGBT section of the Library, and laid a wreath at the War Memorial in honour of Alan Turing and other LGBT war heroes.

Meanwhile CAGS has continued to flourish, and promote new ventures including fortnightly lunch meetings for the over-50s ("Silver Rainbow") in partnership with Age Concern, and bi-monthly speaker meetings at the Brief in George Street ("The Brief Encounter"). Membership numbers, while not up to the level of the Star Disco days, are more than twice the 1983 level, and the group looks forward to its 40ᵗʰ birthday.

To contact CAGS, write to 3 Thanescroft Gardens, Croydon CR0 5JR, or view the website at **www.cags.org.uk**.

Chapter Seven
Annual Gay Events in London

Gay Pride

by Peter Tatchell

Back in 1972, I was 20, with long curly hair, and living in Shepherds Bush with my 17-year old boyfriend, Peter Smith, a student. He was a budding jazz guitarist. We smoked dope and tripped on acid. There was no HIV. David Bowie was the latest pop sensation. Life was a party, up to a point.

In those days, queers were not free. We had to fight for our rights. I was a member of the Gay Liberation Front (GLF)—the first movement of openly lesbian, gay, bisexual and transgender (LGBT) people. We did not plead for law reform. We demanded queer freedom. GLF had a slogan: "Gay is good." These three words were a revolution in consciousness. Previously, nearly everyone—including lots of LGBTs—saw gays as mad, sad and very, very bad.

To combat the invisibility and denigration of queer people, GLF decided to organise a Gay Pride march, with the theme of being out and proud. This was a very radical idea. In those days, nearly all LGBT people were closeted and many felt ashamed of their sexuality.

Not surprisingly, only 700 people joined the first ever Gay Pride march in Britain, held in London on 1 July 1972. Many of my friends were too scared to march. They thought everyone would be arrested. We weren't arrested, but we were swamped by a very heavy, aggressive police presence. They treated us like criminals.

Prior to this, however, GLF had had a march through London in 1971. It started with a small rally in Hyde Park and then a march down Oxford Street and Regents Street to Trafalgar Square. There were about 200 there and a very large number of police. A Canadian called Warren Hague spoke to us and told us about the North American experiences since Stonewall—they seemed to be streets ahead of us at that time.

To return to 1972: despite the police intimidation, we were determined to have a fun time and make our point. The march was a carnival-style parade, which went from Trafalgar Square to Hyde Park. There were lots of extravagant costumes and cheeky banners poking fun at homophobes like the morality campaigner Mary Whitehouse.

We got mixed reactions from the public—some hostility but predominantly curiosity and bewilderment. Most had never knowingly seen a gay person, let alone hundreds of queers marching to demand human rights. "Aren't you ashamed?" one man shouted. "No!" we shouted back, as we blew him a kiss.

Unlike nowadays, there was no festival or entertainment after the march—just an impromptu "Gay Day"—a sort of D-I-Y queer picnic. Everyone brought food, booze, dope and music. It was all shared around. We played camped up versions of party games like spin-the-bottle and drop-the-hanky. I won one of the games and my prize was a long, deep snog with Thierry, a gorgeous French gay activist from Paris.

But it was more than good fun: same-sex kissing in public was in 1972 illegal. Our party game was a gesture of defiance. The cowardly Metropolitan Police would have arrested us if we were lone gay couples kissing, but they dared not arrest 700 of us.

Not everything achieved

In the last four decades Gay Pride has grown from one march with less than a thousand people to two dozen nation-wide parades with a combined attendance of over 250,000. But there are still injustices to overcome, such as homophobic bullying in schools and the bans on same-sex marriage and gay blood donors.

So, celebrate and enjoy Pride, but also keep fighting to overturn these last vestiges of homophobia.

Peter Tatchell

Our thanks to Peter for the above.

*The next two sections are a joint effort by
several friends giving their recollections.*

How Pride Changed

The London gay marches had begun in November 1970 when 150 men turned up to walk through Highbury Fields in North London.

Two years later the first official London Gay Pride march was to be held on 1ˢᵗ July 1972 (the nearest Saturday to the anniversary of the already famous Stonewall riots of 1969). It attracted 2,000 people altogether but the numbers on the actual march would have been smaller, beginning with a rally in the West End of London and finishing with a big party and picnic in Hyde Park.

However it did not seem at first as if the success of the first one would be continued for long after, and numbers declined each year through to 1975 with only 200! In 1977 things picked up again with 1,000 lesbians and gay men taking to the streets—although it is interesting that in the events of '77, according to *Gay News*, drinkers outside the gay pub in Earls Court, the Coleherne, threw beer cans at the demonstrators.

It was ironic that the advent of Mrs Thatcher in 1979 and her attack on gay people with Section 28 seemed to act as a catalyst for Pride, and during the eighties numbers picked up hugely. In about 1983 it was renamed Lesbian and Gay Pride and by the early nineties had become a kind of carnival event, not dissimilar in some ways to the Notting Hill Carnival.

In 1985 there was in fact a water carnival on the Thames with the drag-artiste Divine symbolically shouting at the Houses of Parliament from a launch nearby. In London the Pride of 1988, with anger against Section 28 mounting, had a huge attendance. This continued to rise until 1994 when some estimates put numbers at 150,000.

Fairs after pride rallies

There was nearly always some kind of fair after the Pride rally. In the seventies and eighties this had been held at the University of London Union (ULU)) in Mallet Street. References have been made to the delights of swimming there, when swimwear was optional!

By the late eighties the fair was held annually in Jubilee Gardens on the Embankment. In about 1989, however, it was switched to Kennington Park in South London which was a popular and convenient location, although rather cramped. To give more space, in 1993 it switched to Brockwell Park just south of Brixton, a delightful location with a lot of space, and the half mile route from Brixton tube station to the park developed into rather a march in its own right! Locals used to come into the fair and there never seemed to be any trouble with them. Local kids could be seen playing outside the tents in a relaxed and normal way.

In about 1999 it changed, for about two years, to Clapham Common, then Finsbury Park for one year and finally to Victoria Park for one year— a picturesque location in East London although not quite so good for public transport as the others. We used the word "finally" in the last sentence, as from then on (after about 2003) there was no "big park" gathering afterwards—just the fair in Soho and Trafalgar Square itself.

University of London Union building (ULU)

CHE Winter Fairs

Ian Buist starts:

CHE London held various fund-raising events, principally the annual Winter Fair at Conway Hall in Red Lion Square, Holborn.

Wandsworth-Richmond CHE took part in that first one when they organised a records stall. The event as a whole raised £750 gross. In 1974 they offered to take on the task of organising the whole Winter Fair (23 November) at Conway Hall. Most of the work fell on the shoulders of Vic, a businessman of much enterprise, assisted by Eddie Smith. Thanks to their leadership and personal efforts, and to everyone's cooperation, the Fair raised the huge sum of £1,729, with a net profit of over £1,400—over twice the previous year's net takings. Though not a CHE group, WAGS took a stall (organised by Mike Holden), and there were contributions from other non-CHE organisations and businesses. 1,200 people paid for tickets, and the evening disco was a complete sell-out.

Peter Robins recalls that at the first Winter Fairs there was a real fear that there would be an invasion of straight trouble-makers, wanting to break the whole thing up. Such a fear seems strange to us today, but you must remember that this (November 1972) was one of the first advertised and openly gay events ever, and they just didn't know how the public was going to react. In fact, says Peter Robins, the only invasion was a horde of local ladies coming in at the end to grab all the bargains!

The Marypad CHE group also had a stall at the event each year, originally selling house plants but later on selling magazines (unwanted *Zippers* and *Him* for example), and bric-a-brac.

Malcolm Malins tells us that one year the Marypad group, perhaps unwisely, volunteered to look after the catering, providing teas and coffees and light salad meals from the small cramped kitchen at the Conway Hall. The CHE event was in the main hall but adjacent to the kitchen in a smaller hall was some sort of tropical fish fanciers meeting. They needed to fill their fish tanks with water from the kitchen and were constantly interrupting the caterers. "Perhaps we should have offered fish and chips on the menu," says Malcolm.

The Winter Fair in November 1975 included a very successful disco and a play by Gay Sweatshop entitled *Mr X*.

Griff Vaughan Williams continues:

CHE and GALHA combined to run the Winter Fairs at the Conway Hall, because GALHA was able to get a discounted fee at the Hall. Through the annual winter fairs organised by the various groups in London, and supported by those from the home counties, we were able to raise enough funds to pay the rent of CHE's London information centre at 22 Great Windmill Street.

The demise of the CHE winter fairs in about 1985 was due to the decline in the CHE groups in London (with the reorganisation), and the difficulty of funding the cost of hire of a venue and paying for extensive publicity and advertising.

When there were so many local CHE groups they acted as their own loudspeakers, broadcasting to all and sundry about their participation in the Winter Fair, and with individual groups running stalls. County Hall, with the support of Ken Livingstone, was the venue for revived "Winter Pride" in 1986, 1987 and 1988, sponsored jointly by CHE and GALHA.

The final two Winter Prides were held in 1989 and 1990 at ULU) (which had been the "end venue" for many Summer Prides back in the seventies and early eighties).

Ross Burgess adds:

A memorable feature of Winter Fairs at ULU was the nude swimming: separate sessions for men, women, and TVs/TSs (how do you recognise a nude transvestite?). At the men's session I recall that the showers were used for more than just showering.

Editor's note:

Our thanks to the late Bob Cook, Roy G and Brian Parker for their help in remembering the dates and venues for this chapter, as well of course to the main contributors: Ian Buist, Peter Tatchell and Griff Vaughan Williams.

Chapter Eight
The Harrow Group 1972–

by John Graves and Doug Pollard

The Harrow group started as a branch of the Gay Liberation Front (GLF), a radical organisation without a formal structure. People would meet each week and have noisy debates, usually culminating in a decision to organise some kind of demonstration or protest.

At most GLF meetings, there was a lot of talk, but not much by way of action. Doug Pollard and Suki Pitcher, GLF members, met at one meeting, forming a friendship that has lasted ever since. They decided to start a local branch of the GLF and announced their first meeting, at Suki's parents' home, about a week later. There were four people there—Suki, Doug, Alex (who is still a member of the Group, after 36 years), and Ian.

They placed an advert in the local paper, and from there the group began to grow. Suki and Doug had trouble trying to persuade any pub to hire a room, but they finally found the well-named pub in Wealdstone called "The Goodwill to All", near the Kodak factory.

The Goodwill to All, Wealdstone

From discussions with locals in the bar, it was established that if you are out, honest and open with people, you can do more for acceptance in one-to-one conversations than any amount of speech-making. A key principle of the GLF was the expectation that, if you were not already out, you should be working towards it.

But from the start there were two factions in the Group. Doug was more radical, wanting everyone to come out, to write letters to papers, to put up warning posters in public toilets, to politicise the debate. Most people, however, just wanted a social group—after that became clear, Suki and Doug left and got involved in launching *Gay News*.

Harrow Gay Unity

The Group soon reached out to the other prominent gay organisation at the time, the Campaign for Homosexual Equality. Adopting the name Harrow Gay Unity (HGU), the Group now began to attract a large and regular following and would meet in the bar at Harrow Leisure Centre.

In a way the Group became too large and successful for everybody's liking—as the Leisure Centre management, feeling possibly that HGU would put off others from using their facilities, or perhaps out of sheer prejudice, invented some trumped-up story as an excuse to ban the Group from meeting there.

North West London Lesbian and Gay Group

For a while HGU met, once again, in local friendly pubs. Its name changed, again, first to Harrow and Brent Lesbian and Gay Group, and then to North West London Lesbian and Gay Group. It had its own written constitution, and an elected committee.

In the 38 years that the Group has been around, the world has changed enormously for the lesbian, gay, bisexual and transgendered (LGBT) community. We now have Civil Partnerships in the UK, and the Equality Act. But there is still much to do.

North West London still needs a group that provides a friendly, caring and supportive environment for its LGBT community. The Group informs its members on issues relevant to them, organising talks and discussions, and supplying readily available literature. It seeks to combat isolation and discrimination within the local LGBT community, supporting over seventy members, whose ages range from 20 to 70-plus.

The Group's website gets over 200 hits a week, and in 2006 it received a lottery grant from Awards for All. Finance is still an issue for the group and it is actively seeking support from funding bodies, statutory, public and private, to enable it to continue to build more bridges.

In 2010 the North West London Lesbian & Gay Group is meeting every Monday from 8:30pm, at Tenterden Sports Clubhouse, Preston Road, Wembley. Anyone wanting information can contact the group on e-mail: **nwllgg@hotmail.co.uk**. It is very heartening to think that through all the changes of location and personnel, the group that began about 37 years previously is still going strong.

Tenterden Sports Club Pavilion, Wembley, where **NWLLG** meets

Congratulations to the Harrow group on being one of the first gay groups to have had its history already available on the internet.

Chapter Nine
Jewish Gay Groups 1972–

The first Jewish gay group

D Michael Brown tells us that the first Jewish gay group came out of GLF, (although another one followed shortly afterwards).

He says that there had been several religious gay groups coming together in GLF to make a forum, but inevitably there was a feeling that Christian groups were dominating proceedings. Eventually someone said to those Jewish members who were not impressed with the way things were going: "Well if you're not happy with things why don't you form your own group?" And that's exactly what they decided to do. They started to hold their own meeting at Hillel House, which is the meeting place for Jewish students, but at the same time they kept their links with GLF

Michael remembers how he and Simon Atkins held a one day conference with speakers, including Antony Grey (who had been president of the Shaftesbury Society before it became the Homosexual Law Reform Society with its offices in 32 Shaftesbury Avenue). Another speaker at the day conference was Ian Harvey, the former MP who had fallen foul of the law and whose autobiography was called *To Fall Like Lucifer.*

The Jewish Gay and Lesbian Group

The JGLG started shortly after the group mentioned above, and is now the longest surviving Jewish gay group in the world. According to its website it was founded in 1972 when a small advert in *Gay News* attracted the astonishing total of 190 people to a public meeting called to set up the new organisation.

Since then the Group has gone from strength to strength; in 1993 it co-hosted the 13th International Conference of Gay & Lesbian Jews, and in March 1997 it held its Silver Jubilee Celebration weekend. Both events were attended by people from all over the world.

Membership is open to Jewish men and women who are gay, lesbian or bisexual, and has a wide age range, including people from many different backgrounds, both religious and non-religious.

The Group aims to provide an atmosphere of friendship and support for Jewish gay men, lesbians, bisexuals and their partners; to organise social, religious and informative events for members and guests, and to act as ambassadors between the gay world and the Jewish world, trying to dispel ignorance and prejudice.

Gay people like others are sometimes guilty of anti-Semitism, and the Jewish community sometimes has limited understanding of what it means to be gay. Yet the two minorities have much in common and both face the hostility of extremist groups.

Jewish gay men and lesbians frequently face a lack of understanding, and even hostility, when they come out to their parents and their wider family. Young gays and lesbians may be ostracised for not fitting into the expected pattern of family marriage and parenthood. JGLG offers a relaxed and supportive environment for all ages.

The Group provides regular services taken by rabbis, followed by a buffet, and special celebrations to mark the Jewish Festivals including Seder night for Pesach, and social events for Purim, Rosh Hashana and Chanuka.

JGLG can be contacted at BM JGLG, London WC1N 3XX, e-mail: **info@jglg.org.uk**, web: **www.jglg.org.uk**.

Chapter Ten

The Wandsworth-Richmond Group 1972–1983

by Ian Buist

The first group in South-West London

Early in May 1972 a TV programme went out which gave some publicity to gay issues and, I believe, may have mentioned CHE as such. I wrote to several of the local Putney churchmen to draw their attention to the programme, and got surprisingly sympathetic replies. My own minister (of the Presbyterian Church—now URC Putney) even offered the church as a venue for any meeting which a local group might hold, and said he would resign if the church over-ruled him! The vicar of Putney, Jurgen Simonson, and the local Methodist minister were also welcoming, as was the minister of St Columba's, Pont Street (Church of Scotland).

On 5 September 1972 a first meeting was held, at the instigation of Fred Green, to set up a local group, with nine people attending. Fred agreed to act as Convenor and I as Secretary. We had guidance notes from central CHE on such matters as dealing with the Press and the legal position over recruiting age limits (18 had become the age of majority, but 21 was the legal age of consent for gay men).

We were able to call the first real meeting for 28 September, at a club in Hotham Road, Putney, which hoped to make money from the drinks bought and so did not charge us for the room. We publicised the new development by following up my earlier letters, also approaching the Samaritans and the local Putney Council of Churches. Peter Hain, a Putney resident, already a Vice-President of CHE nationally and then a leading light among the Young Liberals, sent us a message of support. We issued a Press handout to the local papers, and this got publicity in the *Wimbledon News*, the *South Western Star*, the *Mitcham News & Mercury* and the *Richmond & Twickenham Times*.

CHE central office circularised 56 members in our catchment area to let them know about the group. The initial mailing list soon rose to 82, and 35 people attended the launch meeting. Campaigning and social activities were both discussed from the start, and a Treasurer elected (at first Bill Greenhall then Charlie Micklewright). Campaigning focussed first on seeking a change in the age of consent to 18. The first social event was a wine and cheese party.

The Editor comments:

I remember attending the early W-R CHE meetings at the club in Hotham Road: at one meeting in the club someone from the CHE Executive told us we probably had the best meeting place of all the London CHE groups at that time. Sadly, however, in January 1973 the club at Hotham Road decided that it no longer wanted us, as the studios had been rented by a film company, so we had to move to the upstairs room at the White Lion in Putney (close to the Thames and now called Walkabout).

White lion still safe on the roof! The Putney pub's first floor room was used at different times by Wandsworth-Richmond CHE, GLF and WAGS.

The newsletters for October and December show that the group hit the ground running. Apart from lobbying local MPs on the consent issue, we got in touch with the Directors of Social Services for three Boroughs, circulated notes to some 160 local doctors, and planned fortnightly meetings (one a month to include business) for some time ahead. In November Fred got the group "recognised" by the CHE National Council. Our leaflets were made available to libraries in each Borough.

The group also took part in the London-wide CHE Fair in November 1972 at Conway Hall, and actually took over the running of the one in November 1974.

Political Progress

We had secured our first outside speakers in Stephen Kramer, the Liberal parliamentary candidate for Twickenham, and Rev Frank Himsworth, leader of the Putney Samaritans.

Later we were able to move meetings to 51 Sheen Rd, the premises of the RCVS, and an upstairs room at The Imperial, one of Richmond's gay pubs.

At the turn of the year 1972, Fred Green had decided that he wished to move on and I was elected as Chairman in succession. Dermod Quirke took on the Newsletter, and Graham McMurdie the Social Secretary's job. Among newer members we had full-hearted help from Vie and Enrique, Bob Baird became Secretary (Charlie being now Treasurer/Membership Secretary). Mike Turner-Holden[10] added greatly to our strengths, and before long he had started a complementary group in Wimbledon which was not formally part of CHE.[11] Both Mike and I felt it was extremely important to keep a close link between ourselves and WAGS, and he was a member of our committee as well as theirs during the early years.

WAGS later succeeded in getting their MP, who was also Attorney-General, to meet them and hear their concerns about the law. I was able to attend this meeting. I felt we did not really make the most of the

---

[10] Referred to elsewhere in this book as Mike Holden, which was also his stage name.

[11] There is much more about him in the chapter on WAGS.

opportunity, perhaps because some of those present felt so strongly, and some of course supported other political parties and let it show.

However, it was a coup (we had agreed not to give the meeting any publicity) and showed openness of mind and courtesy on his part which were very welcome. Thanks to what I had learnt from Ike Cowen, I was able to correct the Attorney-General on a point of law—an unusual experience for someone with no legal training!

From the outset there was concern that Wandsworth-Richmond was not catering adequately for gay women. This issue was pressed by CHE's first Annual Conference at Morecambe (1973). We felt in our group that to attempt to give our activities a special bias toward women would be counter-productive. Instead we attempted to address this by getting two of our few women members to start up a Women's Group (March 1974). But inevitably, given the focus on legal and similar changes, far more men than women formed the W/R membership. This was the general experience throughout CHE. By mid-1975, however, we were able to co-opt Jean Dodd onto our Committee, and held a special meeting addressed by four women which was well attended also by men, so things were looking up.

One very important meeting later in 1973, with 40 attending, was to hear Sir Hugh Linstead, former Conservative MP for Putney and a member of the original Wolfenden Committee. He had defended its then controversial recommendations in a notably civilised speech in the House, and was able to explain to us why, for instance, the Committee had recommended 21 rather than 18 as the age of consent (it was to secure greater support, with fewer dissenting opinions from members, and because 21 was then the age of majority and marked the end of most men's National Service).

We also had a highly entertaining talk from Dr Rundle, Liberal member of the GLC for Richmond, in August 1974 (he had already said he favoured an age of consent of 16).

Making Waves in Richmond

Our outreach strategy was to establish ourselves firmly as reputable actors on the local scene, and to spread the word about the need for equal treatment as widely as possible. This also meant countering all the usual misconceptions. We therefore applied to join the Richmond Council for Voluntary Service (there was no similar body in Wandsworth, but we made comments on the borough's 10-year plan for the social services).

We were called to an interview with some of its Committee. The fiercest inquisition came from an older man whom afterwards we learnt to be a closet gay! After we had assured them that our membership was restricted to those over 18, and that we would not sell *Gay News* on the premises, we were accepted.

Belonging to the RCVS allowed us to rent a room for meetings in Richmond, to play some part in its work, and to advertise ourselves to other voluntary organisations.

Over the next two years we were able to give talks to, among others, the sixth form at Rutherford School, students at Whitelands College of Education (whose lecturer in health education also came to talk to us), the Hampton Association of University Women, Richmond Young Conservatives (twice), and students at Guy's Hospital (on "the normal homosexual"). We also held a meeting with the local Chief Inspector in Tooting, and addressed Hampton Wick branch of Twickenham Labour Party.

In late summer 1975, at John Middlebrook's suggestion, a group was formed of a few members willing to give help to the Multiple Sclerosis Society in Richmond. Local publicity on this was coupled with the report of a successful representation by the Group to the MPs for Putney and Twickenham to ask them to press for discussion between the Attorney-General and the DPP on the use of "conspiracy" charges against papers publishing same-sex contact ads.

For both the General Elections in 1974, W-R conducted a survey of candidates' attitudes towards law reform, and circulated the results to members. We also attempted to lobby during elections to the GLC and local authorities. We publicised national and London-wide activities as well as those going on locally. Social functions were organised with other groups, particularly Streatham CHE.

Outreach

Early in 1974 Jack Ellis, one of our group, and Eddie Smith, a Committee member, arranged to provide Richmond Library with *Gay News* for a trial six-month period. But in September, despite the periodical having been in constant demand, the Council's Amenity Committee decided to discontinue taking it, while simultaneously agreeing to keep the National Front's publication, *Spearhead!*

We set about campaigning to get this decision about *Gay News* reversed. After seeing the Librarian, we tried in vain to get interviews with the Councillors responsible. We therefore wrote formally to the Librarian, quoting the responsibilities of the Council under the Public Libraries and Museums Act, and lobbied Council members outside their meeting place at York House. All but three accepted our letter. The story was carried prominently by the Dimbleby Press (the *Richmond & Twickenham Times*), and we wrote letters—published—to reinforce this. There was a very supportive editorial. (Arthur Godfrey, chief reporter for the Group, had also given us a talk in May 1974.)

In addition to our monthly meetings, Dermod was able to get us occasional lettings in libraries under Wandsworth Council, and we had a few successful Saturday discos at the library in Latchmore Road in the late seventies (including a disco on St Valentine's Day, which happened to fall on a Saturday in 1976).

CHERP!

Early in 1976 I was promoted to a post which involved continuous absence at many international meetings at which I had to represent Britain. I could no longer therefore carry on as Group Chairman or Convenor. Jon Child was elected in my place, and remained there until early 1978 when Tony Konrath, previously Campaigning Secretary, took over. The Group was rechristened "CHERP", which recognised that the balance in members had shifted more towards Richmond than Wandsworth (but "P" was for Putney).

I was able to help in a few ways, e.g. by hosting a small party at my home and by taking part in a presentation on CHE's work to the RCVS, along with Tony and Jon (July 1977). The Group continued to play an active part in the Winter Fair.

Membership continued to rise, and discos staged by CHERP were very profitable. But there was less support for the ordinary meetings and social get-togethers. So in 1983, following the collapse of the system of CHE groups, the decision was taken to merge CHERP and CHEK (CHE Kingston) to form KRAGS, the Kingston and Richmond Area Gay Society.

Several members of CHERP, such as Tony Konrath and Jack Ellis, went on to play a part in the newly formed group. Readers can find out, in the chapter on the Kingston Group, how things developed with KRAGS.

A final view of Richmond

We are very grateful to Ian Buist for the huge amount of information provided for both this chapter and for the one on CHE London.

Chapter Eleven
London Friend 1972–1979

A gay-led counselling and befriending organisation

Manchester Roots

Friend was founded in London and Manchester in 1971 as a befriending offshoot of the Campaign for Homosexual Equality (CHE). CHE was campaigning for equality but members soon recognised that there was a need for a telephone help-line and social support groups to help those who were isolated and coming-out. They took referrals from the CHE headquarters in Manchester and the Manchester University Homophile Society.

A national network of volunteers soon evolved and at its peak Friend had 21 groups around the UK and Ireland. Friend nationally set out guidelines for the operation of the local groups and monitored standards. Each group was an independent body with its own patrons and support groups and offered a range of services appropriate to the needs of its local community.

Friend in London

Mike Launder, a Camden social worker and activist within CHE, led the formation of London Friend, which at first operated from the Earls Court flat of one of the founders but was soon receiving so many letters and phone calls that it moved to a community centre in Church Street, Westminster. In 1976 the Chair of London Friend, New Yorker Jack Babuscio, who had witnessed the Stonewall riots, published a book *We Speak for Ourselves* which stressed the need for social services and counselling organisations to be more aware of the presence—then often hidden—of gay people, and of our needs.

In 1975 London Friend secured an Urban Aid Grant from the Home Office, supported by Islington Council. It was the first ever government grant to a gay-led organisation and was then considered so controversial that the Home Secretary, Roy Jenkins, personally steered the grant through.

Friend in London and elsewhere attracted national press comment in those days, with as many as fifty phone callers an evening and befriending/counselling groups on most nights.

London Friend moved to shop front premises at 274 Upper Street with offices and counselling rooms above, and for the first time took on a full-time paid administrator, Roland Jeffery. At this time there were about 70 volunteer befrienders. The Islington Premises were opened by Graham Chapman, from the Monty Python team. He was called in at the last moment because special guest Maureen Colquhoun MP, who lived locally and who had intended to make her coming-out speech at the open event, bowed to her party's pressure and cancelled.

London Friend's old HQ in Upper Street, Islington

A developing Identity

London Friend's phone help-lines provided help with coming-out and other gay issues to callers from across London, and were backed up with free face-to-face counselling, support groups for young and for older people, and a library of gay and lesbian books. Much of what it did was referred to as "befriending". This was not just a play on the organisation's name, but an attempt to avoid the perception of medical or therapeutic overtones. Many people who contacted London Friend had no social or emotional problems beyond the refusal of society—as recently as the 1970s—to accept gay people, our sexuality and relationships. What Friend in London and elsewhere provided was a place where people could overcome such hostility, encourage their self-esteem and overcome the stigma that many still felt.

In selecting befrienders, the organisation did not require formal qualifications, and, though some gay people brought us complex problems, in some cases requiring legal or medical referral, many were merely isolated or damaged by social attitudes to their sexuality. What they needed most was the re-assurance they could get from meeting their peers: self-confident lesbians and gay men whom they could talk to freely and in confidence.

Calls to the London office came from across the UK, especially when London Friend used some of its grant to advertise its service in the national press, including the *Daily Mirror* and *The Sun*. To some it must have seemed safer to call about gay issues from Scotland than to phone a local help-line where you might be identified. We even had calls from Australia! All callers could remain anonymous if they wished, but if they wanted to meet face-to-face, they were given the contact details of a Friend group nearer home.

Organisations such as London Gay Switchboard (then the largest in the world) and Icebreakers were often the first point of contact for lesbians and gay men coming to terms with their sexuality. These organisations would often refer callers on. Gay Switchboard specialised in keeping a huge database of information, from flat shares to the addresses of gay pubs and hobby groups; it also operated 24 hours a day. Icebreakers was another befriending group, not dissimilar to Friend but with a stronger emphasis on befriending and a dislike of more formal counselling which they felt had overtones of stigma.

So, as large numbers of lesbians and gay men were becoming more open about their sexuality and relationships, so too were gay-led organisations developing their identities and profiles.

There was national press coverage when London Friend provided a poster to advertise its service in Islington Borough's public lavatories—in those days numbering 32—alongside posters for STD clinics. Some gay people thought this presented a poor stereotype of gay people as lonely and desperate, but the response on the Friend phone lines showed the advertising reached many who were married or who did not identify themselves as gay.

London Friend also started taking trainee social workers who earned their professional qualification, in part, by supervised placements at Friend. This was at a time when gay and lesbian social workers could—and did—lose their jobs for being open about their sexuality, and was the cutting edge of changes in the social work profession. But in spite of paid staff and professional trainees London Friend was—then as now—an organisation largely run by devoted unpaid volunteers.

After the Urban Aid grant ran out London Friend survived on volunteer labour only before being funded for many years by the London Boroughs Grants Unit.

The 1980s

The 1980s saw an explosive growth in the visibility of gay men and lesbians in all walks of life. Some of the hard-fought victories of the gay activists in the 1970s were now bearing fruit in this decade, though it was soon marred by the terrible onset of HIV/AIDS. It was becoming far easier to lead a gay lifestyle, especially in London. As a result large number of lesbians and gay men chose to move to the capital. This kept Friend busier than ever, as newcomers, often escaping to what they saw as a new life in a gay-friendly environment, were brought up short by the pressures and problems of urban life and relationships.

Many gay men were happy to enjoy the growing commercial gay scene that rapidly developed in the 1980s. Clubs and bars for lesbians were also opening, though in much smaller numbers than their male equivalent. In London, some might find going to a gay pub or disco frightening; London Friend therefore started two social support groups: one for young men, and Junction for mature men. These were running in 1975 though not under the same names. Also there were many more social groups and non-commercial activities in the 1970s and early 1980s. *Gay News* was full of listings for special interest and social groups.

Turning points

Turning Point was established as a coming-out group for men who were gay, or thought they might be, and this broke new ground by meeting initially in other premises, and by having a rolling programme of topics on gay life. You could start anywhere on the cycle and stay through to the end. Some even went round twice! While Turning Point still meets, the group for young gays became redundant as more of them found it easier to come out as gay. The group for older gays continued for a long time, then went into hibernation, and has recently been resurrected as Mattrix.

Friend members also started the Older Lesbians Network; after it had been running for a long time, it seemed right to encourage it to start an independent life. In the same way, a small group for gay prisoners provided support within prisons by sending gay newspapers and writing letters, until it too achieved its independence. We also used to answer letters from people looking for support in coming out—a medium now entirely replaced by e-mail and the internet.

We were asked to help train police cadets at a time when most gays did not trust the police to be impartial. Friend volunteer Matthew Windebank was booed when he gave his first session at Hendon Police College but he returned and persevered, and awareness of the rights of gays and lesbians became an integral part of Metropolitan Police training with Matthew playing a key role in its development.

For many years, London Friend has had a banner and we have marched behind it at Pride. There were even specially printed T-shirts and badges for participants in the early days. We were very proud one year to be encouraged by our Chair, Ian Ferguson, who was on duty in his police uniform.

After a change of ownership our Upper Street premises were becoming dilapidated, but we were a sought-after venue for other groups to meet. In the 1970s gay theatre group Gay Sweatshop had rooms in our building as an office for its touring.

The London Bisexual Group met on Friday evenings and the London TV/TS group was successfully established during our time in Upper Street, meeting every Saturday and Sunday night. They were glad to be able to bring their frocks in a suitcase and to change at London Friend before their meetings. Our phone-workers were glad too, as TV/TS organisers always brought cups of tea or coffee up to the phone room for those doing a shift on those weekend nights. The Beaumont Society, successor to the London TV/TS Group, still meets at London Friend.

London Friend separated legally from CHE in 1975 when it became a non-profit company. By the mid-80s a lengthy process updating our constitution began, ultimately qualifying us for charitable status. London Friend's time in Upper Street was brought to an end by galloping inflation of house prices in London in 1986. Our building was sold twice in six weeks, each buyer putting up our rent until we could no longer afford to stay.

We moved temporarily to offices above the Cheltenham & Gloucester Building Society in Seven Sisters Road. While there we started an ambitious project to set up a group for gays and lesbians with mental health problems. We appointed a qualified nurse as our co-ordinator but, despite his considerable efforts, we discovered that mental health patients did not want to attend a group exclusively for them. Then we discovered that Circle 33 Housing Trust had gone beyond the terms of their lease in subletting these rooms to us and we had to find new premises urgently.

Up to the Present Day

In 1987 we found our present home in Caledonian Road, with the help of Islington Council who rent the premises to us. There was a bureaucratic hiatus in preparing the lease, resolved only when we wrote directly to Bob Crossman who is remembered as the first "out" gay Mayor of any UK local authority.

Our Treasurer had cleverly managed to salt away any surpluses over the years, so we had enough money to cover the cost of installing central heating and building the coffee bar.

London Friend's present headquarters, Caledonian Road, 2009

We appointed two part-time co-ordinators to develop our services. We set up a support group for women coming out and Changes is still meeting this need. Evergreens was started as a social group for older men, and Lesbians at Friend on Sundays (LAFS) for older women.

Fusion was a successful social support group for gay men of different ethnic origins. These ran for many years.

Our face-to-face counselling service was reorganised to include an initial exploratory assessment followed, if appropriate, by 12 weeks of counselling. Realising that clients valued the professionalism of our counsellors, we started asking for a donation for their service. This seems to have reduced the number of missed sessions too.

London Friend's financial security was threatened some years ago when the London Boroughs Grants Unit decided to concentrate its funding for gay and lesbian work on one organisation, and it wasn't us! Fortunately we received substantial bequests in the wills of three generous people and have been living on these.

Training and support

London Friend has tried to support our volunteers over the years with both in-house training and social occasions.

We filled the Conway Hall and recruited some expert speakers for a training day on AIDS in its early days. More recently we had good attendance at a training event we organised on transsexuals. MIND came to speak to us about mental illness, LGCM talked about gays and Christianity, and the Beaumont Society told us about its activities for TV/TS people.

Recent ventures are setting up Artworks for gays and lesbians, and taking over the Lesbian & Gay Bereavement Line, which runs every Tuesday evening. In partnership with the Metropolitan Police we encourage reporting of homophobic and transphobic crimes. With NHS Islington Primary Care Trust we he set up a Stop Smoking Group and with MacMillan nursing we run GMAC, a cancer support group for gay men. Fusion, a new group for black and ethnic-minority lesbian and bisexual women has recently started.

London Friend also provides a venue for Lesbian Alcoholics Anonymous meetings and for Stonewall Housing interviews.

Adding to this history

If you had contact with London Friend in the early years, as volunteer, befriender, somebody for whom Friend provided valued support, why not get in touch. We will respect confidentiality if you wish to remain anonymous. However we would like to add to this account of the organisation and the struggle for the social acceptance of gay men lesbians and our relationships over recent decades. Please e-mail us at **londonfriendhistory@mac.com**.

London Friend Today

London Friend is now the oldest established LBGT charity in London. London Friend has no political affiliation and consciously recruits both male and female volunteers, though there is always a criterion that volunteers are themselves LGBT people. London Friend continues to function from its address in Islington, North London. Full details of its activities can be found on the website (**www.londonfriend.org.uk**) and it can be contacted at: London Friend, 86 Caledonian Road, London N1 9DN, or by e-mail at **office@londonfriend.org.uk**.

Editor's note:

This brief history was prepared in February 2009 by Roland Jeffery and Dugan Cummings with assistance from Alan Swerdlow, Chris Payne, Robin Bloxsidge and Tom Rowbottom. © Dugan Cummings and Roland Jeffery.

Chapter Twelve
The Lewisham Groups 1972–1985

CHE and other gay/lesbian groups in Southeast London

by Trevor Denham

Until the 1970s Lewisham and South East London had no gay pubs—the nearest were the Union Tavern in Camberwell New Road and the Kent Arms, North Woolwich—and the only other meeting places for gay men were cruising areas in a few notorious parks, cottages, and local authority Turkish baths. Lesbians were no better served.

The Borough of Lewisham in the early 70s became a launch-site for groups addressing various gay/lesbian-related issues. An informal weekly meeting of gay men from the St Katharine's group who lived in South East London started in 1970. Integroup, also started in 1970, met monthly in a non-conformist church with the aim of establishing better understanding between gays and others. Another voluntary organisation started locally at that time was Parents Enquiry (founded by Rose Robertson), which offered support for parents of gays and lesbians, and later took on a national role.

Lewisham CHE

Early CHE groups established in London were all in the central area. The first "local" London group was established in Croydon in 1971, and this was used as a model for a group of CHE members living in South East London to start a local group based in Lewisham early in 1972. They were joined by some SK members and there were also direct referrals of new members joining national CHE plus the Lewisham Group's own advertising.

By 1975 CHE Lewisham had a programme of activities taking place several times a week in various parts of South East London. The group started organizing larger-scale events. There was a memorable Christmas party with pantomime in 1975 and a fund-raising Mardi Gras Fair in March 1976. Some of the money raised went towards making an amateur film called *David is Homosexual*, which was filmed in the summer of 1976 and first shown in 1977.

The main meetings were by then held at the Lee Centre, which was used by a wide variety of community groups.

The Lee Centre where the Lewisham Group held activities

David is Homosexual was used as a campaigning aid, and was shown around the UK including at educational courses. Up to this point there were few positive images of gay people in the media; television showed considerable interest in our film, and Channel 4 and the BBC went on to make their own programmes reflecting gays more positively.

In its early days the Lewisham CHE group had little success in attracting lesbians. Later more women started joining national CHE as it became more active politically, and the membership of CHE Lewisham gradually reflected this.

In fact the Lewisham group developed a reputation for activism. Its banner was always to be seen on Gay Pride marches. On 13 August 1977 CHE Lewisham's banner formed a focus for gays and lesbians marching against the National Front in the demonstration mounted by the All Lewisham Campaign Against Racism and Fascism.

Members of CHE founded a number of spin-off activities for gays and lesbians, notably Lewisham Friend, for counselling and befriending, which existed for about 20 years, and a weekly disco called "Saturdays", which ran for several years in a local pub.

Setting up other gay groups

By 1976, with well over 100 members from a catchment area of at least four London boroughs, the Lewisham group decided to encourage the setting up of more CHE groups in other Southeast London boroughs.

The first step was to encourage local gatherings, and out of these came the CHE groups in Bexley (which ran a highly successful local disco for several years), Bromley and Southwark/Lambeth. Later a small group of Lewisham members started a separate lesbian and gay group in Greenwich which set up the Greenwich Lesbian & Gay Centre, and this eventually developed into the Metro Centre.

One of the main functions of CHE groups, including Lewisham, was to break the ice for gays and lesbians who were previously isolated. At the same time there were members for whom activism was highly important. Friendships and partnerships were formed which in many cases outlived their membership of the Lewisham group

2LGA

In the mid-80s the Lewisham CHE group started losing momentum. Its social activities were outclassed by the growing commercial scene of London's gay pubs and dance clubs, and it also found it difficult to attract committed leaders.

The Group therefore closed down in the mid-80s. Some of the core members kept in touch—they are still in contact today—and in 1991 they started a new organisation, when Lewisham Gay (later Lesbian and Gay— 2LGA) Alliance was formed. It worked closely with Lewisham Council as a campaigning and project group. It was involved in healthy lifestyle issues with weekly fitness sessions and made history when it was awarded substantial Government funding from the Home Office's Safer

Neighbourhoods Unit to produce the first report in UK on violence against gay men, published end of 1991.

Not old fuddy duddies

John Mathewson describes how he came to join Lewisham CHE:

My first experience was in the mid 1960s with the Homosexual Law Reform Society who had offices in Shaftesbury Avenue. I think it was run by Guardian-reading type straight people (anyone who was gay couldn't openly admit it before the 1967 act anyway). As I told them I wanted to be cured they sent me to a Harley street psychiatrist who charged me a whole week's wages just to tell me I could be normal if I thought of women in trousers when I masturbated.

By 1972 I managed to make a few gay friends, one of whom found out that GLF had weekly meetings in the public library in Knatchbull Road, Camberwell, so we went along several times. It was indeed most liberating to sit in a circle (so no one person is the head) with a crowd of other gay men—many of whom would become part of the famous Railton Road Brixton collective. But the meetings we went to at that time appeared to be all talk and no action, although later on they put on some most enjoyable dances in Fulham Town Hall, where once again we'd often dance round in big circles—great fun. It just shows how open minded some Councils were even in those days (Hammersmith and Fulham for Fulham Town Hall, and Lambeth for the use of the library). So much for the so-called loony left!

But at the weekly meetings the gay libbers would often make jokes about CHE, specially the Lewisham branch, who according to them were a load of old fuddy duddies who wanted to change society's treatment of us from within the system.

So one Monday evening I went along to one of the Lewisham CHE meetings in St Lawrence's Church Hall, Catford, just to see what it was like—and I joined immediately! I just felt so at home. Two men who were partners, Trevor & John, had started the group I think about six months to a year before I joined.

Most people (mainly men) joined Lewisham CHE for social reasons, but its aims were also political—acceptance of equality for gay men and women: for example making the film called *David is Homosexual* about a young man coming out as gay, and getting it shown in several local schools.

Editor's note:

We should pay special tribute to the excellent and almost unique work that the main Lewisham group did in helping neighbouring areas to set up groups.

The Libertines Group in Lewisham 1980–1999

By Dave Latchem

Libertines was one of the very first groups started by an outside organisation, in this case Age Concern. It was originally called the Over Fifties Gay Group. Ralph Berkett (a straight person) was the development officer of Catford Age Concern and he was able to obtain a grant for them to start a group for older gay men.

Fun and games at the "pop in parlour" in Lewisham

In the local papers there was an angry response from local conservatives protesting about the use of ratepayers' money for such a project, but Dave wrote in a letter pointing out that gays paid rates just like everyone else. Having written the letter he then decided he ought to join!

He became Chair, a post which he held for six years. During that time the group became involved with SLAGO activities. He did not agree with the change of name to Libertines but he went along with the decision. Chas and Wendy took over, when he insisted he needed a break. Reg Jones of the Croydon group was also involved.

Libertines met fortnightly in the Pop In Parlour, a Lewisham coffee bar. About twenty were on the books and about eight attended each time.

The group was disbanded in about 1999, but they have many happy memories of events held. The photo on the previous page shows a very convivial evening when they held a birthday party for the president and ate his head! Don't worry—the rest of him is still there under the table!

Chapter Thirteen

A Miscellany

We are putting some groups together in this chapter, not because they are unimportant or even small, but because we don't have a huge amount of information on each of them.

Coming out of their shell: Ealing (EGG) 1980–

Neil Henderson recalls how he came to live in Ealing in 1972 and soon settled in with his partner Peter Knight (now sadly passed away). They were both fairly new on the gay scene and had tentatively joined groups, described in past chapters, such as St Katharine's and London Monday.

Neil remembers Ealing CHE being formed towards the end of 1973 and as far as he recollects it just met in members' homes. The group folded after only a short time but several of its members started another group in Ealing called "Challenge" in 1975. In February 1980, Challenge merged with Chiswick CHE to become "EGG"—the Ealing Gay Group—which explains the title above! Unlike most of the groups founded at about the same time, EGG was always a social group only and never got involved in campaigning. In the diary for 1980, for example, the group visited Heaven (the big disco up in town), had a fancy dress tea party and made a trip to Kew Gardens. Occasional speakers came to the group but meetings were nearly always held in members' homes. In October 1980 Neil remembers the first cheese and wine party which he and Peter held in their flat with great fear and trepidation. But it was very successful.

A bi-monthly newsletter was established, which has continued ever since. By 1985 the membership had risen to around 100. A regular event was the pub evenings at the King's Arms, where Desert Island Discs was very popular. A two day trip was made to Bournemouth. Visits to the Stallions Tea Dance in Charing Cross were also popular on a Sunday in the late eighties, and pub visits to the well-liked Penny Farthing in Hammersmith were well attended.

EGG continues to offer a relaxed social group for men living around West London. Anyone who would like details of current EGG activities is invited to visit the EGG website at **www.ealinggaygroup.org.uk**.

The Octopus Group 1982–

Octopus started in Chelmsford in the late 1970s. It was called Octopus as it was "sending out its tentacles" into remote parts of Essex but also into part of East London. In this respect it has much in common with Magnet, which was based in Kent but started activities going in the boroughs of South East London, notably Bromley. In 1982 Octopus was set up formally, with weekly meetings in members' homes. Parties have always been well attended and a Eurovision song contest party was particularly successful. The 25th anniversary party in 2007 was very well attended indeed.

If anyone living in our area would like to join they would be made very welcome. They can go to our web site at **www.octopusgroup.org.uk**.

The Walking Group

The CHE walking group is now the Gay Sunday Walking Group. There were probably two other such national, but London-based, groups. They were the Motoring Group, and the Music Group (known as Allegro). People heard about them mainly through word of mouth.

The walking group was founded by Vivian Waldron, at that time a recently retired senior civil servant and a leader in the hiking group section of the civil servants social club. Vivian led the group on the walks he had taken the civil servants on, starting in 1972 with a walk in the Sevenoaks area. If any member of the public asked who they were and why they were all gentlemen Vivian insisted they told them clearly "We are the Campaign for Homosexual Equality Walking Group" A friend and founder member of the walking group said he first heard of CHE from a letter in *The Guardian*.

Pimpernel 1984–1999

Based on conversations with Alex Duncan

Pimpernel is the exception to most of the groups in this book in that it was under the umbrella of a sympathetic but non-gay organisation, namely Age Concern. They held weekly meetings at the Age Concern day centre near the Oval.

There would be tea and coffee with a weekly average attendance of about twelve, although there were about sixty on the books. Occasionally there would be a birthday party when the lucky member would bring in a birthday cake and everyone else was encouraged to bring a bottle.

Peter Robins, our chairman, had a lot of connections and was able to get some really good speakers, such as Peter Tatchell and Richard Kirker, as well as a famous ballet dancer or opera singer. Sometimes we would have a bring and buy sale, and at Christmas everyone was encouraged to bring in something to eat—it was always a marvellous spread.

Following the demise of Pimpernel, a number of its former members were involved in the setting up of Just Friends, which has a wide variety of interesting speakers and other events.

Naturist Groups

By Ross Burgess

For a time in the late 20th century there were at least three London-based gay naturist groups. London Gay Naturists (LGN) had regular naturist social events, Gay London Swimmers (GLS) had swimming sessions at various venues, and Gymnos offered both social events and swimming. Rules of etiquette varied between the groups. LGN strictly forbade sexual activity at its social events, while Gymnos took a more relaxed attitude. The one rule common to all three groups was that trunks etc were banned.

All three groups have now ceased to function. The social events probably ceased because fewer people were coming forward to host them, and commercial venues offered naked parties, while the swimming sessions were affected by the closure of older local authority swimming pools, as well as the shortage of members to act as lifeguards. More modern pools tend to be more open to view from outside, making them unsuitable for nude swimming. Particularly sad was the refurbishment of ULU), which made the magnificent pool visible from the reception area, and thus put paid to any further use of the pool for naturist sessions.

Chapter Fourteen
The Streatham Group 1972–1986

*Based mainly on notes provided by Iain McDonald, convenor
of the Streatham Group for several years until 1982.*

Setting up the group

Although meetings of the group are believed to have started in October 1972 (just a few weeks after the Wandsworth-Richmond group), the Streatham group appears not to have been formally founded until December 1972. On the 14th November 1973 a constitution was adopted for the group at a meeting which was informally chaired by Ian Clayton, and held at Clapham Park Library. The adoption of the constitution was celebrated with a dinner-dance at the Queens Hotel, Upper Norwood, where the entrance price was £3.25.

Over the next five years there would be a number of convenors, all of whom made significant contributions, including Doug Randall (who has sadly now passed away), Clive Ransom and Nick Winterton. Francis Howard was Honorary President from 1975 to 1980.

26 August 1977 saw the publication in the *Streatham News* of a double centre-page spread about Streatham CHE. This was a very important event for Iain McDonald. It was after this, in September, that, with some trepidation, Iain and his partner Ken set out to their first Streatham CHE event—a Sunday tea at John Craig's! With John's friendly welcome, all those other lovely people and all that fantastic food, how could they refuse to join? Of course, they did join, and Iain was persuaded on to the committee at the December 1977 AGM. He duly became Social Secretary, a job which usually strikes fear into the heart of anyone asked to do it—certainly the effect it had on him.

The overall story of 1977–79 was, in many ways, one of continued growth and success for the group. The initial number of members is unknown, but the membership grew to over 175 towards 1982. A very impressive number even for those days!

Campaigns and public events

Campaigning activities continued in varied ways—for example in June 1978 four members of the group addressed a meeting of the National Housewives' Register, and in October 1978 five members addressed Tooting Labour Party. A vivid memory of the event is that the Party stated its commitment to equal rights, but then all of the women got up to make the tea during the break!

In July 1978, a questionnaire was sent out to 102 family doctors in the area. Most of the 26 who replied had what might be called an enlightened attitude to homosexuality.

In October 1978, a Book Campaign was launched; this was one of the most important projects undertaken by the group, and it was still going strong in 1982. It monitored the content of books for stereotypes of lesbian and gay people, and challenged authors and publishers to change them. In addition, in February 1979, the group's library was formed and Edward Brink later became the librarian. The first edition of the leaflet "Is there gay life in Streatham?" was produced in August 1979. The group held an exhibition of gay literature, photographs and press cuttings for a week in Streatham Library in July 1980.

In July 1979, the group exhibited at the Lambeth Country Show, held in Brockwell Park, for the first time; the group's stand, in the open air, was a great success. We again exhibited at the Show in July 1980, but this time we had a stand in the local groups' tent—for which we were grateful, as it poured with rain!

The month of October 1979 saw the end of a long battle to gain membership of the Lambeth Arts and Recreation Association (LARA). The whole saga occasioned the group's first appearance as headline news on the front page of the *Streatham News*. Subsequently, LARA was wound up. In August 1980, the group also joined the Wandsworth Legal Resource Project, the first gay group in the country to be involved in such a project.

Newsletters were produced from the beginning, but January 1974's newsletter is handwritten. The first printed newsletter was produced in March 1974; it was originally named Strenews. In June 1976 the Newsletter suggested the formation of small special interest groups for various sports, pub crawls, etc, which became a regular feature.

"We are the Sub-Aqua Group"

Back to the earliest days. In August 1975 meetings had been started at a room in Streatham Baths, close to the well-known Streatham ice rink. These group meetings, held on Fridays, were called "Club Night".

Steve Harrington remembers attending one of the very first meetings at Streatham Baths, with his older friend Iain MacEwan, a veteran campaigner and member of the old Homosexual Law Reform Society. Steve distinctly recalls that when they arrived at the reception of the Baths they had to say they were members of "The Sub-Aqua Group." The story reminds us of how discreet gay meetings tended to be in the suburbs.

Streatham Baths, where first meetings were held

Presumably, with some of the speakers being respected local personalities, gradually such "closetry" as in the last paragraph became unnecessary. The first politician to give a speech at these meetings was in fact the late Marcus Lipton, then MP for Lambeth Central, and who was there again in August 1976.

In October 1976, one interesting meeting was addressed by a member of Alcoholics Anonymous, who gave a speech on the "The Homosexual Alcoholic". And another meeting was addressed by a member of PIE (Paedophile Information Exchange), who gave a speech on "One Paedophile's Experience". Subsequently, however, the group tended to shy away from this subject.

Meetings at Streatham Manor Hall

In August 1977 the venue for the meetings was changed to the Streatham Centre (Manor Hall) behind Streatham Station. Speakers in the first six months included John Fraser, MP for Norwood, the Prices and Consumer Affairs Minister in the Callaghan Labour government, Margaret Drabble who famously described how difficult it was to write about cosy domestic gay life without seeming coy, and Polly Toynbee, a *Guardian* and *Observer* columnist who was formerly the BBC social affairs editor.

April 1978 saw Jilly Cooper, then of the *Sunday Times*, visiting Nick and Phil's house to talk to members of the group. A full feature in the *Sunday Times* was the result! This was followed by Denis Lemon, editor of *Gay News*, and then a hilarious evening was provided at Manor Hall by Margaret Powell, who was something of a cult figure as well as the author of *Below Stairs*, a famous book at the time. In August 1978, the speaker was Ted Knight, then a rather notorious Leader of Lambeth Council, followed by Derek Malcolm, *Guardian* film critic. Alf Dubs, MP for Battersea South, also spoke to us in November 1979.

The meeting of 30 January 1980 was an evening to remember! The speaker, Rev Eddie Stride, Rector of Christchurch Spitalfields and vice-chairman of the National Viewers' and Listeners' Association, requested that we did not throw things at him during the meeting (as if we would!). Apparently this had happened to him before—not entirely surprising in view of the opinions he expressed. We were "moral poison", he said—and that was one of the nicer things! We still didn't throw anything.

Simon Callow, the actor, spoke to the meeting in March 1980; Richard Balfe (our Euro MP) and Peter Katin (the famous pianist) both spoke to meetings in April 1980. Barry Protheroe of the National Council for Civil Liberties spoke to the group in September 1980, and Maureen

Colquhoun, open lesbian and former Labour MP for Northampton, spoke to the group in December 1980.

During 1981, the speakers included Helen Shapiro, Sandy Wilson, Kenneth Williams (who gave a bizarre talk on medical ethics—not at all what members had expected), Chad Varah (founder of the Samaritans), and local Liberal candidate Tim Clement-Jones. Also there were speakers from the Gays in Housing Group and the Gay Teenage Group.

During 1982 the speakers included Julie Walters who was predictably hilarious (and during the meeting discovered she had trained at the same hospital as one of the group's members), as was Miriam Margolyes, whose talk was so outrageous no part of it could be reported to the local paper!

Social Activities

During its existence, the group organised many social events, some of which are described below.

In October 1973 a neighbouring group, Wimbledon Area Gay Society, was founded, and Streatham members attended at least one of the WAGS discos at the brilliantly named British Queen public house in Haydons Road, around April 1974. These were later moved to the Royal Standard at Colliers Wood where members continued to attend sometimes

A joint social with the Croydon and Lewisham groups was held in June 1974. And in the same year members were offered winter breaks to Paris, Copenhagen, Amsterdam, Hamburg or Benidorm by the CHE Travel Service. Streatham CHE also hosted discos at Liberties in August 1976.

During 1977 the social programme took off under John Craig's direction, and in every month there were theatre or opera visits and social evenings, and our famous Sunday teas first made their appearance.

Landmark events

March 1977 saw the presentation *An Evening of Words and Music* at the Bedford Park pub in Streatham, performed by Carol Boyd (famous as Lynda Snell in Radio 4's *The Archers*), John Craig and Mark Bunyan. Roy G tells us that Mark and Carol were a wonderful act together! It was an unforgettable evening, and raised £50—a lot of money then—for the *Gay News* Fighting Fund against the Mary Whitehouse blasphemy prosecution.

By the way, the group used to go to the comfortable Bedford Park pub after most of the speaker events, since the Manor Hall was a bit Spartan. (Sadly, at the time of going to print both the Manor Hall and the Bedford Park pub appear to have closed.)

The group's first jumble sale in April 1977 also raised £100 for the *Gay News* Fighting Fund. Other jumble sales were held in July 1980 and in November 1980, raising £290 and £141 respectively. Another jumble sale, held in St Leonard's Hall, was also a bumper success, raising over £275. Twenty-five members were involved in running it at a time when the group's membership was only sixty!

On 15 July 1978 the group had its first coach trip, to Oxford, Woodstock and Blenheim.

In December 1978, the first disco organised by Streatham CHE, the Snow Ball, was held at the Surrey Halls in Stockwell, and was a great success. Following this success, the group held a second disco, Snow Ball Two, in December 1979. It made a profit of £100, donated to Friend. The most successful event of 1981 was the disco held at the Phoenix in Cavendish Square, where 150 people attended

Notable events of the years 1979 to 1980 were evenings where members invited relatives to a social gathering, and which were known as Parents Evenings. Mothers, fathers, sisters and brothers were all welcome and the evenings were a great success.

Not quite so serious as the above, in September 1979 the group visited the Gay Wrestlers Group[12] at Streatham's own Manor Hall.

Last years

In the first ten years of its life, Streatham CHE had achieved a huge amount. Over the years, members of Streatham CHE went on to found,

---

[12] Unfortunately, this is all we know about the Gay Wrestlers Group, except that they also gave a talk to the Marypad group! Ed.

for example, Gaycare, the Gay Humanist Group (later GALHA) and the Gay Social Democrats. A member, Francis, joined CHE's Executive Committee. All these were considerable achievements.

In 1982 the Streatham group looked forward to the next ten years in a spirit of great optimism, but sadly this bright future was not to be. CHE as an organisation of gay groups fell apart at about this time, and the Streatham group (officially called Streatham CHE) changed its name to the Streatham Area Gay Group (SAGG).

What led to the end of the group's life? Key to its closure was that a wonderful guy called Ian Parkes, who used to arrange all the speakers, moved away. Once they no longer had him to organise all the speakers, the group's attendances died off very quickly. Perhaps people had not really been interested in the group as such, but attended because they had such marvellous speakers? Attendances fell to as low as three every fortnight, until in Christmas 1985 the clause in the constitution was invoked for the dissolution of the group.

A Special General Meeting was called for the purpose and the group was dissolved. The last meeting in 1986 was attended by only three members, one of whom (Stuart Draycott) had been doing most of the committee work single-handed for some time; there seemed little support for any continuation. However, a good number of former members of SAGG joined CAGS at that time, and some have remained members to this day.

Several of the group's members are still in touch with one another, and there was quite a reunion at the celebration of Iain McDonald and Ken Thomas's civil partnership in Exeter in 2008!

Who would have thought such a thing possible back in 1972 when the group started?

Editor's note:

Our thanks to Iain McDonald and also to Stuart Draycott, for their help in giving us information for this very interesting chapter.

Chapter Fifteen
Icebreakers 1973–c.1984

*Our thanks to Jeffrey Weeks for letting us include
a chapter from his excellent book Coming Out.*

The most radical community-based support organisation was London Icebreakers, a phone service for isolated homosexuals set up in Spring 1973.

Icebreakers began with the principle that what the most isolated, unhappy or even desperate homosexuals wanted was not "expert advice" but the simple affirmation of their identity and sexual orientation. Icebreakers made a point of telling their callers that they were themselves homosexual, and that this was a source of pride for them, not shame. The phone number was widely advertised through stickers, advertisements in the gay and alternative press, and occasional articles in the orthodox press, and there was an immediate response.

Icebreakers received from 4,000 to 5,000 calls a year, about one in six of which were from women. One in ten callers were married, and one in twenty calls were from transvestites. The callers covered the gamut of sexual tastes, class and age range (eleven to seventy). Problems varied from loneliness to difficulties of youth and age, of relationships, of being married and gay, and of being religious and gay. What most callers had in common was a sense of isolation—either physical or of their inability to speak of their problems to family or friends. An ongoing contact with Icebreakers provided a lifeline out of this loneliness.

To complement the phone service and to provide a more personal forum than the phone could offer, a regular Sunday afternoon social for men and women was begun, and this proved enormously successful, with sometimes thirty or forty people coming to the socials in homes of individual Icebreakers. Later a similar fortnightly meeting especially for lesbians was started. At those meetings callers could discuss their particular problems and begin to build up personal links of friendship and support. Icebreakers' organisation kept itself deliberately small with a collective of about thirty, as it was keen to keep democratic and community based.

Despite its straightforward approach, Icebreakers aroused a great deal of controversy, especially in its rejection of the role of individual counsellors. The Albany Trust in particular, which had devoted a large part of its urban aid grant of £30,000 to training counsellors, was outraged, and sharply criticised Icebreakers for being "silly" in its attitude towards experts. But at stake was a whole policy of homosexual politics: the Albany Trust remained wedded to a position of "supportive neutrality", whereas the gay liberation organisations were increasingly committed to a policy of positive espousal of gayness.

Icebreakers in theory went beyond that in stating their adherence to a wider political position that gay liberation proper could only come with the breakdown of rigid divisions and the transition to a new society.

From a dangerous to a safe headquarters

Thanks to Nettie Pollard for helping us gather information for this part.

At first, in 1973, Icebreakers was situated at Branksome Road, Brixton, in a hostel for young homeless run by Roger Gleaves, the "bent Bishop of Medway". He was later imprisoned for his part in the murder of a young runaway, which eventually became the subject of a TV documentary called *Johnny Go Home*. (The title was based on the even more famous documentary of seven years previously called *Cathy Come Home*.)

Icebreakers became deeply suspicious of what was going on with the bishop (it was probably a phoney title in a dubious church), and started to suspect him of abusing the youths in his care. So they were grateful to Micky Burbidge, who managed to move them quickly into a squat in Railton Road, perhaps number 155, a first floor flat about half a mile down the road from Brixton on the left.

The GLF place, which eventually turned into the South London Gay Centre, was not far away, but closer to Brixton and on the other side, perhaps at number 78: it had two floors with a coffee and discussion place in the shop, and discos downstairs in the basement. There was bound to be a lot of contact between the two Railton Road squats with so much in common—for example, Bill Thorneycroft of Icebreakers was also very involved with the South London Gay Centre.

Chapter Sixteen
Quest 1973–

by Michael Stephens

Early in the summer of 1973, a young Welsh Catholic in London who had been inwardly agonising over the conflicting demands of his homosexual urges and the teaching of his church, plucked up the courage to consult a priest. At the local presbytery he was met by the curate, not many years out of the seminary. Talk was easy, until the main matter at issue was introduced. It quickly became plain that the priest was wholly unfamiliar with the subject and pastorally quite unprepared to guide and counsel any homosexual people. His eventual recourse to a textbook on ethics yielded no illumination, and the young man left in a mood of anger and frustration.

Still in this mood, he placed an advertisement in the personal column of *Gay News*, the fortnightly journal for homosexual readers: "Will any Catholic interested in meeting to discuss the Church's attitude to homosexuality please write to Box ..." With the publication of this notice, he unwittingly planted a seed whose sapling—ten years later—had established firm roots in the soil of Catholic Britain.

Seventeen replies were received, all but two of them from the London area (where *Gay News* was, in those days, much more easily obtainable), and all from men. On 6 November 1973 nine of the respondents assembled in London for the inaugural meeting of what the convenor chose at the time to call the Catholic Gay Caucus.

Four initial objectives had been proposed for the group in the convening letter, each suggested as the main topic for separate meetings:

1) Discussion within the group about the attitude of the Church towards homosexuality (personal views and problems etc);
2) Education of the clergy by personal contact and correspondence;
3) Education of Catholic press (not allowing outbursts of "anti-gay" to go unanswered);
4) Allowing clergy to use the group name as a means of publicising "pro-gay" literature.

The first topic proved an effective one for an opening meeting since, given the opportunity to talk about his own experience, each began to get to know something about the others. Prayers at the outset and a glass or two of wine as the evening progressed established that atmosphere of serious sociability which has marked the group's meetings ever since. And there was no reluctance when the meeting ended in agreeing a second one two weeks later.

Some time later it was decided, in pursuit of the second initial objective, that each person present should send—not as an individual but as a member of the group—a letter based on an agreed text to individual priests with whom they already had some contact, formal or informal.

Reconciling faith with sexuality

The group, which was soon to abandon the description "caucus" and call itself the Gay Catholic Group, had now drawn up a programme including periodic meetings as well as individual action in the meantime. At this stage it made no deliberate effort to expand.

Meetings were held informally in private homes in different parts of London at roughly monthly intervals. At some of these a priest or other concerned person was invited to initiate discussion. No records were kept; no structure was required. But a growing sense of purpose and of commitment shaped the small band into a more and more self-accepting, trusting team of faithful Catholics with a shared conviction that, where homosexual people were concerned, the Church had not yet got it right.

In the autumn of 1974 a paper was prepared (with some hope of publication in the Catholic press) which reviewed the group's findings—both in its own discussions and in the conversations with individual priests.

At the outset of these meetings it became clear that, while each member of the group could name several other homosexual Catholics who had totally abandoned their religion on this one account, none of themselves had taken this decisive step—as yet. Neither, however, had any fully resolved the central problem: that of reconciling the practice of their religion and the practice of their sexuality

The partial resolutions of this problem were discovered within the group to have taken one of four main forms. Some had been so discouraged by their experience in the confessional that they had long been deprived of the spiritual benefits of Holy Communion. Others, from a similar experience, had habitually ignored the confessional and continued in conscience to receive Holy Communion. Others, again, had taken advantage of the opportunities for choice of church that city dwelling can provide, to go in for confessional "shopping around" until they had gained the ear of a sympathetic priest. And still others had settled for the performance of an annual ritual penance and Communion while otherwise withdrawing from religious practices.

Few of the priests consulted seemed to have much understanding of the potential capacity of homosexual adults to achieve mature, stable, and indeed moral, Christian relationships.

Expansion

Some contact had already been made with the *Catholic Herald*, and a copy of the Catholic Gay Group's review was made available to the paper. Early in January 1975, Peter Nolan—one of the *Herald*'s staff correspondents, later to become its editor, described how Christians had begun to adopt a new and more compassionate approach to "gay individuals."

The *Catholic Herald* report made the group's existence and objectives publicly known for the first time. And the moment was apt. By the beginning of 1975 the members individually had developed sufficient self-assurance as confessedly homosexual and Catholic people to be ready to move out of the shadows, to which they had earlier felt themselves confined, and into the open. They were now in contact, too, with a number of informed and sympathetic priests who were both willing and able, through this group, to make their good counsel more readily accessible to those in need of it. They felt equipped both to expand and to move forward.

By midsummer 1975 the group had registered just over fifty members, most of them still from the Greater London area, and all but one male. Private homes could no longer easily accommodate full meetings, and it was the group's good fortune that two of its newer members had recently moved into a basement flat in Bayswater. Until they had completed furnishing, their carpeted, floor-cushioned but otherwise largely bare living-room provided space for gatherings of twenty or thirty; and it was at one of these that Fr Michael Hollings first talked with the group.

Fr Hollings was the more open-minded of the two priests whose contrary views had been reflected in the pages of the *Catholic Herald*. Earlier, in 1972, he had contributed to a series of booklets commissioned by the St Thomas More Centre for Pastoral Liturgy, one concerning "the pastoral care of homosexuals".

In 1972, the homosexual societies to which Fr Hollings referred were, in Britain, for the most part entirely secular, and perhaps rather more suspect to the clergy. But the following year, as if by a process of spontaneous spiritual combustion, saw the formation not only of the Catholic Gay Group, but also of the Friends Homosexual Fellowship, the Jewish Gay Group and the Methodist (later ecumenical, and now defunct) Open Church Group. These groups added a new dimension to the scene, for they were concerned not so much with bringing homosexual people together "within homosexuality" as within the context of their own faith. And pastors like Fr Hollings welcomed opportunities to meet with them.

St Mary of the Angels

Across the road from the Bayswater flat where the Catholic Gay Group was meeting stands the Church of St Mary of the Angels, well provided with several spacious parish rooms. Evidently encouraged by his encounter with the group, and aware—for the meeting at which he spoke had been very well attended—of its need for space, it was Fr Hollings who persuaded a priest at St Mary's to offer the group houseroom for future occasions. The two members of the parish invited this priest to the next gathering, and by May 1975 the parish rooms of St Mary's had become the group's regular meeting place in London.

The first informational news-sheet, distributed to members in June 1975, records as its first item: "At the meeting held at St Mary's on Sunday 11 May it was decided to change the name from "Catholic Gay Group" to "Quest: a group for Catholic homosexuals" (Quest for short). With its emphasis not so much on the composition of the group but on its pursuit, the title has well stood the test of time, and what may have seemed at the time to be almost a casual choice has proved to be something of an inspired one.

St Mary of the Angels, Bayswater, where Quest held meetings

The group now had both a name and—for its principal London meetings—an address; for postal communications and enquiries, the domestic address of its secretary was published wherever opportunity allowed. "Secretary" because during this period, with the general approval of the members, a small central ad hoc committee had been composed to direct the group's development.

Discussions with guest speakers at now regular monthly meetings at St Mary's were central to the programme, but, although there were opportunities for informal talk over coffee afterwards, it was recognised that for many apprehensive and shy newcomers an initial plunge into a large and somewhat formal meeting was not the best introduction to Quest. Members who had the facilities, therefore, were encouraged to be 'at home' to others whenever they could.

Mention has already been made of the development of an informational news-sheet distributed to all members. Its potential, however, as an instrument for bringing even the most isolated member into some sort of contact with others was quickly apparent, and the second sheet—covering the two months of August and September—announced that "Plans are in hand to produce a Quest Newsletter which will not only carry the sort of local information included in this news-sheet but also other reading matter that it is hoped will be of interest and help to gay Catholics anywhere".

Early in 1980 Quest bought a quarter-page advertisement in *Gay News* to declare "News for gay Roman Catholics." Quoting the pamphlet, the advertisement announced that: "Your priests are now publicly being told that as a group that has suffered more than its share of oppression and contempt, the homosexual community has particular claim upon the concern of the Church. Quest continues to urge and argue this claim within the Church, with increasing support and in more and more places. Come and join us."

In March 1980 Quest proposed, in a letter sent to all the area bishops in the Westminster diocese, the holding (it was hoped during Gay Pride Week in late June) "of a public service in Westminster Cathedral ... that sets out specifically to attract the attention and engage the participation of homosexual people."

Awareness is usually best achieved through witness; early in 1981, following consultations with the regional convenors, the national committee began laying plans for "a series of public meetings centring on a scripted presentation of some Catholic responses to questions about homosexuality."

The notion was that the "scripted presentation"—which in due course emerged in the form of a one-act play—could be transferred from place to place, be presented either by a touring cast or by members of the various regional groups,. It would be supported by a local panel of Catholics able to answer questions and stimulate debate. *Gate Thirteen, a comedy-tragedy-thriller-fantasy* was presented in the Manning Hall, London University Union, on 28 November 1981 before an audience of 60 or so.

Linkline

Fr Hollings suggested that he might squeeze Linkline into some shared accommodation in his Bayswater presbytery; and a Catholic organisation based within walking distance of the Earls Court underground came forward with the option on exclusive use of a good-sized upper floor room in its own house. The October Newsletter announced that: "Friday 6th November 1981 is the date on which Quest's own switchboard will open."

"After many months of searching, praying, planning and training, we have—in the Linkline—reached what will be seen as quite the most important landmark in Quest's history—a service that will at last give more of those many hurt and hesitant gay Catholics whom we have not yet reached easier and anonymous access to us and to that sharing of experience that enriches every life."

On the evening of Friday 23rd October, in the church of St Mary of the Angels, Fr Michael Hollings was joined by several other priests in concelebrating a Mass both in thanksgiving and in further spiritual preparation for the opening of Linkline. Some fifty members of Quest took part and joined in the social that followed in one of the parish rooms.

Exactly two weeks later, one of the volunteers picked up a ringing telephone receiver and for the first time spoke the friendly words that have been uttered hundreds of times since: "Quest Linkline. Can I help you?"

From 1973 to the present day Quest continues to expand and thrive, and has groups and contacts throughout the UK. For more information please see **www.questgaycatholic.org.uk** or the Quest Linkline, 0808 808 0234 (Sunday, Wednesday and Friday, 7–10pm).

Chapter Seventeen
WAGS (Wimbledon Area Gay Society) 1973–1995

by Geoffrey Leigh and Tony Walton

Friends and neighbours

Tony starts:

A small group of Wimbledon gays, Mike Holden amongst them, had become members of the Wandsworth-Richmond CHE Group over in Putney. The Wandsworth-Richmond Group suited us fine and we liked it a lot, with Putney only fifteen minutes by bus from Wimbledon. But just a few months after it started, the Putney club where we held our meetings told us they could no longer have us there.

For a while the group changed to the upstairs room of the White Lion, Putney, but then, disappointingly for us, moved to Richmond. I say "disappointingly" because getting from Wimbledon to Richmond takes forty minutes, twice as long as central London, and for us it was no longer "local". So the obvious thing was to start having meetings in Wimbledon. We had by this time all met Geoffrey and John, a couple who lived locally.

Geoffrey continues:

Well, WAGS (Wimbledon Area Gay Society) all began in our front room in October 1973. My boyfriend, now my husband, John and I agreed to hold a social in the front room of our first floor Victorian flat in Woodside, a residential street in Wimbledon. The room was big and could easily accommodate twenty but as it was we got a hell of a lot more in. All very noisy, crowded and great fun. The purpose was to set up a group for local gay men and women. This was following the problems there had been in GLF (we had been members) and in a new spirit of wanting to do things locally. For many gays, local was scary—you went elsewhere for pubs and clubs—nothing local where you could be identified by neighbours, work colleagues, family etc. However, people were enthusiastic by now for a local group if only to meet other people.

At one of the early meetings Professor John suggested we should call ourselves WAGS: not just because of what it stood for but also because it sounded a fun name—we all roared with laughter when the name was agreed!

Creating a scene

A deliciously outrageous and lovely guy named Mike Holden became chairman and the public face of the group. Some artistic members created a banner, with the motif of "togetherness":

We took it to most of the early gay pride demonstrations, with Mike shouting out some very frank gay slogans in his booming voice at all the watchers on the pavement!

Mike had appeared on TV as an actor in a play called *The Owl Service* and as one of the lads in *Please Sir!* By the time we knew him he was moving on to work for *Gay News* with Denis Lemon. After this he helped to start the newspaper called *Gay Week* with a group of friends.

Tony continues:

WAGS was one of the community gay groups which sprang up in the early 1970s. I had joined the SK Group in 1968 and WAGS in 1973, but the contrast between the two was enormous—a contrast explained by the huge shift in public attitudes in those years.

I suppose that the advent of GLF during the five years had made a real difference. GLF, with its completely "no holds barred", incautious and fearless approach to gay matters, had made an impact on even the most timorous. "If they can get away with carrying on like that, why do we need to be so timid?" was how your average gay reacted, even if they thought GLF was sometimes over the top.

We were also bold enough to want to improve the local gay scene. One quick and easy example: there was no gay pub in Wimbledon. OK then, we said, let's all meet at the Alexandra, just north of Wimbledon station, every Sunday lunchtime and turn that into a weekly gay pub. Lo and behold, within a few months the Alexandra was listed in the gay papers and gays were flocking from all over South West London to socialise there.

Anyone who has been on an assertiveness training course, or a life-coaching course, will know that one of the aids to keeping sane and balanced is to say the magic word NO! And I really think that looking back on the history of WAGS if we had learned occasionally to say no, life would have been a lot less stressful. So this is how things used to go in WAGS (led by Mike) over the next two or three years:

Shall we start a weekly gay disco? Yes ... Shall we start a monthly serious meeting? Yes ... Shall we start a *daily* gay switchboard service? Yes ... Shall we start a monthly lonely hearts meeting? Yes ... Shall we attend the annual CHE conferences? Yes ... Shall we support Gay Pride events? Yes ... Shall we take a stall at the CHE Winter Fair? Yes ... Shall we do some local campaigning and persuade the local council to give us a grant? Yes ... Shall we start a women's disco? Yes ... Shall we run a monthly newsletter with info about the gay scene and ideas as well as just a programme? Yes ... Shall we change a local pub into a gay venue? Yes ...

I'm not saying that WAGS worked harder than other groups—I am sure many other groups worked harder and were under similar pressure—I am just saying if WAGS had tried to concentrate on slightly fewer things we might have functioned better! But the biggest pressure of the whole lot, and you'll notice the very first thing in the list above, was the weekly disco ... and in the next section we'll be telling you the whole of that story.

Early discos—and the WAGS' Dunkirk

Geoffrey begins:

Eventually through the auspices of a wonderful man named Eric Buchanan we found a secure place at a pub in Colliers Wood for our discos, named the Royal Standard (Tony will tell you the story of our short-lived *first* disco which preceded that). Eric was in his eighties when he came out after his wife had died, and eventually he allowed his room to be used as the base for our phone service.

Tony continues:

It's worth bearing in mind that the average age of members of gay groups in those days was probably about 35. There was a certain feeling of making up for lost time. Life hadn't been much fun for us when younger because of gayness being illegal, so maybe we were making up for lost time—and discos were something we were determined to organise and to enjoy.

The first venue for our weekly disco in 1974 had been the back of the appropriately named "British Queen" in Haydons Road, on the corner of North Road (the pub was in fact named after an old paddle steamer). One very memorable disco evening there was the May Day special when we had the room done out with red flags and pictures of Che Guevara— there were also camp jokes such as "Dave will be displaying his solidarity later on." Bob Hill, who'd lived nearly all his life in Burntwood Lane not far from the BQ, and who was a lifelong socialist, could hardly believe his eyes when he attended the event. Something left-wing *and* gay in his area?—for dear old Bob it was too good to be true.

And it *was* too good to be true. The disco had only lasted about three months when we started getting bad vibes, with the landlord telling us he wanted to double the price etc. We arrived at the BQ one evening to be told that the landlord could not have us. So we'll now give you a quote from the next WAGS newsletter, to tell you about the drama:

"The saviour of the evening was the landlord of the (mile distant) Royal Standard, with whom we had already discussed the possibility of future meetings … At literally a moment's notice he let us use his clubroom for a disco. Fifty dazed queens were then ferried down to the instant *new* venue together with a large amount of equipment, in an operation resembling Dunkirk."

Rear-view of Royal Standard, with "garden shed" on left

The new place turned out to be a large clubhouse in the back garden of the pub, with its own bar, soon acquiring the nickname of "the garden shed." There was a grand sense of cosy togetherness about the whole thing, even if it was not over-elegant.

But because it was right opposite a tube station, gays flooded in from all along the Northern Line to what quickly became known as one of the friendliest gay discos in South London. By about 9 pm we would be full up and having to refuse entry, so we had to find bigger premises, and the only compensation was that the women members took over the garden shed for a women's night disco.

After about a year at the nearby King's Head pub, a new manager started making problems for us there, so we moved in mid-1976 to the Merton Hall, in South Wimbledon. Numbers rocketed to over 200 and we were amazed by our own success! It was in walking distance of both Wimbledon and South Wimbledon stations, and being in local authority premises seemed to be a symbol of acceptance. We were to stay there for over five years, although not without complications.

Merton Hall in South Wimbledon, with gay discos 1976–81

The Campaigning Side

Geoffrey begins:

In 1975 we decided to set up a local gay helpline, and Mike approached the local council for a grant to get it all started, on the grounds that as gay ratepayers we were entitled to this. Luckily for us there was a wonderful Tory councillor called Ken Goddard who was in charge of the LBM grants committee, and he signified that he would give us the grant.

But at that time Sir Cyril Black had only just retired as Wimbledon's MP, and he was described as "the moral conscience of England." He was now an influential borough councillor, and he set about organising the opposition to the grant.

We all went down to Wimbledon Town Hall (now the front of Centre Court shopping) to hear the debate—Ken Goddard wonderfully using quotes from the bible to out-manoeuvre Sir Cyril, such as: "Do unto other as you would have them do unto you" and so on. We all kept very quiet and well behaved but when the vote was announced, with a majority in favour of the grant, we applauded and were overjoyed.

Tony continues:

Curiously, although we were not a CHE group we were always interested in campaigning. I remember one of our chairpersons, Pam, presenting a wreath at Wimbledon War Memorial for gays who had died in concentration camps—it was quiet but dignified.

As early as 1974 we had held discussion-type meetings with speakers at the Labour Hall opposite the Polka Theatre in Wimbledon Broadway. Speakers included Rose Robertson of Parents Enquiry (helping young gays and their families), Keith Bill the local Labour candidate, and George Nairn-Briggs, a local curate involved in gay counselling. There was also a showing of the CHE education kit for teachers, followed by a discussion on the needs of youngsters at school.

A happy story with a very sad ending

In the mid-seventies Eric Buchanan, mentioned above, was our social organiser and Bob Hill, whom we have also told you about, came onto the committee. Another person whose life was much changed by WAGS was Peter Waggett. (Both Bob Hill and Peter have now passed away so in a way it's easier to tell their story). Peter had lived his whole life in Avenue Road, Raynes Park, with his parents, although he had been lucky enough to form a long-term, loving relationship with an older and kindly gay man named Doug.

A public discussion was held in a Wimbledon church, St Andrew's, prior to the council debate on whether WAGS should have a grant or not. To our surprise Peter's mother stood up to voice her support for the local gays, saying it was time to show more fairness to the thousands of people like her son. It was a dramatic and effective intervention.

As Geoffrey has told you, the WAGS phone service was set up in 1975 and Tommy Jones worked hard for several years as its organiser. He was followed in about 1979 by Ian Johnson, who kept it going very successfully at a member's house in South Park Road.

An elderly gentleman who had joined in 1975 was Dudley Littleton whose house (also in South Park Road) happened to back onto Mike Holden's back garden in the Broadway—inevitable jokes about "fairies at the bottom of the garden!"

Mike Holden at International Gay Rights Conference in Scotland in 1974 ... note the gay badges, one of them WAGS

Mike heard that both Dudley and his friend Iain MacEwan had been keen members of the old Homosexual Law Reform Society, and typically he marched round the corner to recruit Dudley into WAGS. Dudley joined on the spot, telling me afterwards that if all WAGS were half as nice as Mike he just couldn't wait to get involved! Dudley used to regularly give us slide shows about his travels into exotic parts, and these were always popular events at the Labour Hall. Like Mike, he loved the visits after the Labour Hall meetings to George's Coffee Lounge opposite the library, where we would all continue chatting and socialising.

So we must come to the end of the story about dear old Mike Holden. He was chairperson for about three years before he moved over to North London, although he kept in touch with us all and came regularly to the weekly disco, by that time held in Merton Hall.

In the summer of 1977 we heard the dreadful news that he had been murdered. It had nothing to do with the gay issue: he had been drinking with some work friends in a straight pub in Mayfair on a Friday night when a stranger came into the bar shouting. Mike told him to be quiet, and the guy brought down a soda siphon on his head.

I am enclosing part of the tribute paid to Mike in the newsletter, the obituary which Geoffrey and I wrote jointly: "We remember him first for his audacity—totally open about his gayness and turning WAGS into the best known gay group in the country. With his driving force there was never a dull moment and nothing stood still. Secondly we remember him for his great personal kindness—his flat in Wimbledon Broadway was an ever-open haven, and he always had time for all gay people, re-assuring them and caring for them."

My then partner Antony Hardy also says that to this day he feels sad about Mike's end, remembering him vividly as a very beautiful person in every way.

Pioneering Days

Geoffrey continues:

We had so many lovely people in WAGS in those early days. Mike of course whom we've already told you about. But also Ted Wright who was on the door at discos for years (and looking after the younger patrons!). There was also Derek who handled the finances, Tony who was the secretary and kept the show on the road until Win took over, Eric who was nicknamed by Mike as "Eric the half a bee" after a silly song of the time—and lastly Bruce, a delightfully friendly guy from Australia. Also three couples: Dennis and John who had great parties in their home in Trinity Road by South Park Gardens; Ted and Alan, the charming local greengrocers who hosted some of the very earliest meetings at their flat in Edge Hill Court (their shop by the theatre became something of a drop-in centre); and their equally charming friends Doug and Dennis who lived near them.

We had a real sense of community, of not hiding in the closet, of knowing other local gay people and helping each other along.

Tony continues:

And at the same time there were some great days out, so here are a few highlights: In February 1975 we went to Wimbledon Theatre to see maybe the last performance of Marlene Dietrich. Needless to say the audience was full of gays and there was a wonderful atmosphere, perhaps making a final link with the nineteen twenties. Social historians might see similarities between the gay scene in twenties Berlin—"divinely decadent darling!"— and the wild gay scene in seventies London.

In the same year we went to see the Beverley Sisters at the same venue. Then in October 1976 we held our third anniversary fancy dress disco at the Merton Hall. For fringe, we used to visit the South London Theatre Centre in West Norwood and got to see some excellent amateur productions. One month we went to see *Waiting for Godot* at West Norwood and then "the divine Mrs Shufflewick" at Stratford—so we had pretty wide tastes. Another striking theatre visit was to see Lindsay Kemp dancing at the Roundhouse, Camden—and we adored his outrageousness!

A bit less outrageous, we would make occasional visits both to the Streatham bowling alley and to the ice rink, as well as trips to visit the Father Redcap or the Union Tavern in Camberwell.

Terry Noble used to run new members' evenings at his flat in Southcroft Road, Tooting, which helped quite a few still lonely and isolated people find their way into a friendlier society. But there were also some things that would be considered very risqué nowadays—such as going onto Wimbledon Common to visit the Sunday cruising areas. (Mike even put a map into the newsletter to show the cruisiest bits!).

Towards the end of the seventies a strong team had taken over the running of WAGS—Stefan A as Chair, Ian Johnson as treasurer, Win B as secretary, Mike K as phone secretary, Geoffrey Leigh as campaign organiser and David Warner as disco organiser. Ron Aldred, a senior citizen, was one of the leading lights and we enjoyed his stories about Wimbledon's naughty gay life in World War Two.

The serious emphasis was getting involved in the community and forming links. For example I did some work with local churches trying to improve attitudes, bringing together in April 1980 clergy and church leaders in the local boroughs with a discussion at St Andrew's, Earlsfield. Geoffrey persuaded the local librarian to stop preventing serious gay books from being displayed on the shelves, and we also put on a *public* showing of *David is Homosexual* at the Wimbledon Community Centre.

Into the Eighties

The Merton Hall venue lasted altogether for five years from 1976, with Ted Wright as the main organiser, once nicknamed "everyone's Argentinian auntie." It started off as a weekly event and Ted did a great job running it. Occasionally joint discos with the Wandsworth-Richmond CHE were held in a library hall near Clapham Junction, and there was a particularly successful one there on St Valentine's Night 1976—we're told some permanent friendships were made that evening. Occasional Saturday discos were also held, firstly at the Kings Head and then at Merton Hall.

But then in 1978 there was an argument about whether we could be allowed a weekly bar at Merton Hall, since it could only be licensed for occasional use, although I think this was a genuine legal wrangle and not to do with prejudice. In the end it was decided that WAGS could have one disco a month and there would be other gay discos run by different people on other Tuesdays. The monthly WAGS disco on the first Tuesday continued there right up to 1981.

However, for some very strange reason there was a wish to keep holding a *weekly* disco too. We tried the White Lion, Putney but switched to the Wheatsheaf, Tooting Bec (since it was on the Northern Line) every Thursday evening in the upstairs room, with David Warner as our excellent disco organiser. It was a popular venue and we held a successful WAGS fifth anniversary disco there in October '78—numbers reaching nearly 100.

Then we experienced a bad piece of luck: the Wheatsheaf had organised a heterosexual event on a Sunday, and it had all got a bit out of hand, with one of the barmaids being offered as a raffle prize! The brewery reacted furiously when the story appeared in the *News of the World* and the manager was told to close down his upstairs room for *all*.

A number of experiments were started, firstly at the Grove Tavern in Norbiton on Thursdays (the Kingston group were there another evening, and I think the link was Gregory Jotham who was a keen member of both groups). Then we tried two experiments closer to home at the Selkirk Arms in Tooting and the Earl Spencer in Southfields. The fourth experiment was in 1980 on Friday evenings—for the second time in the upstairs room of the White Lion in Putney, where we might well have stayed.

Then rather to our surprise (I think our resident DJ John had a lot to do with it) we found that we would be welcome to run a disco at the Dog & Fox, an extremely up-market pub at the top of the hill in Wimbledon Village, with a huge ballroom and excellent facilities. Wow! Once we had found the D & F, both the White Lion and Merton Hall were quietly phased out—the facilities were so brilliant it didn't seem to matter that it was a long walk up the hill from the nearest underground.

At the same time (we've arrived in our story at May 1981), the licensing laws were relaxed for this type of event, with gay discos for the first time staying open until one in the morning, which of course meant that few people arrived much before ten! As a group we were on average older than we had been in the days of the Standard—it may have been great fun for men in their thirties to be bopping about till eleven at night in the garden shed, but not quite so much fun for those in their forties to be looking after the door at the Dog & Fox till one in the morning, mid-week.

The D & F, however, was a goldmine, and it was hard to let it go once we had started. People streamed from all over London to go there— WAGS was the in-place to be. Vivian was by now the chairman of WAGS with Norman "Smiler" from Surbiton as the very capable disco organiser. Terry Murphy had joined the committee by this time and I had rejoined as secretary again—all trying to keep everything running smoothly.

We were making so much money that there was pressure on us to open a local gay centre in South Wimbledon—and we actually went to look at a shop in Victory Road, in about 1983. I think we just had cold feet about taking over so much responsibility, and a general meeting voted the idea down—very wise probably. (In the 3F chapter, there is a section on the problems that the London Lesbian & Gay Centre in Cowcross Street, Farringdon, had just a few years later, and the Croydon group also decided against opening one about the same time as us).

Problems in the Eighties and Nineties

By the time that the management had taken over the running of the Dog & Fox disco in March 1984 we had made a huge amount of money, which of course meant that South London Gays, the successor to WAGS, started off with a very large credit balance in the bank. Unfortunately however, the actual membership of WAGS in any real sense was starting to decline.

We started the final WAGS disco at Tiffanys, which was part of the Wimbledon theatre complex, but it only lasted a short time, because in all honesty we had run out of energy to run discos. Serious meetings had been switched in 1980 to the Victory in Colliers Wood (now the Colliers Tup) where we had a few very spectacular arguments. One of the most ironic was the huge quarrel in October 1980 about whether we should become a fully-fledged CHE group or not—we had been affiliated since 1978. I say the quarrel was ironic because not long after our discussion the whole national CHE groups structure broke up, with groups such as Croydon and Streatham CHE becoming "area gay societies" the same as WAGS.

For a while meetings were in the upstairs room of the Prince of Wales opposite Wimbledon Station, where we ran our own bar and where everything was fine until we had our stock of beer stolen from the cupboard. It persuaded us in 1985 to return after a break of six years to the Labour (William Morris) Hall, where we started meeting weekly.

Of course AIDS cast its dread shadow over us at this time, as it did over all gay people. At the end of our table tennis tournament in the Labour Hall in 1991 (we had our own table there) the winner's cup and runners-up shield were both purchased and presented by Mr Shearman, whose son had been a member but had sadly died. He made a very moving speech at the end of the presentation. It was indeed a sad era.

Winding down

During the eighties the strain of running both a weekly disco and a weekly meeting meant there wasn't much energy left to do anything else, although we used to have pleasant monthly Friday evening get-togethers, jointly with the other SLAGO groups such as MCC, in the Two Brewers at Clapham.

In 1994 our twenty-first anniversary party was held back at the Kings Head, where a friendlier management had taken over again, and the cake was cut jointly by Terry Murphy and Pam (WAGS' first and only woman chairperson). In 1995, however, it was noted that very few WAGS members actually lived in Wimbledon, and so the decision was taken to make a fresh start—by renaming the group SLG (South London Gays) and by giving the whole thing a completely new beginning, unconnected with WAGS, and looking for new members throughout South London. Our very last outings were trips out with Barry in his vintage bus, which were great fun, and visits to the Kingston Green Fair in Canbury Gardens, where KRAGS had a stall.

So it's completely true to say that WAGS finished in 1995. But it was a pity we missed having a silver jubilee—Mike would have been so proud of us!

Chapter Eighteen
Metropolitan Community Church, London
1973–

The history of the Universal Fellowship of Metropolitan Community Churches goes back to 1968, the year before the famous Stonewall riots, with the founding of the first church in Los Angeles by Rev Troy Perry. By 1972 there were several thriving churches in the USA and Troy Perry was becoming well known, not only as a Christian minister but also as a campaigner for gay and lesbian rights. In that year Troy was invited to London by CHE to address a public meeting in Conway Hall.

At that time there were few support groups for LGBT Christians, and they kept a low profile. But inspired by this meeting, a group of gay and lesbian Christians formed a group called the Fellowship of Christ the Liberator (FCL). This met in a private home in Barons Court for a Sunday Communion service and weekday meetings. The services were conducted by a rota of supportive clergy from various denominations.

First of the few

In October 1973 FCL was chartered as the Metropolitan Community Church of London. It was the first recognised MCC outside the USA, narrowly beating Toronto. This move was not supported by a minority of members who believed it conflicted with their loyalty to their previous denominations, and so a few people left. Some of these went on to be amongst the founders of the Open Church Group and the Gay Christian Movement (now the Lesbian and Gay Christian Movement). MCC London was supportive of these new organisations as they were seen as complementary to MCC's aims. But clergy from the other denominations who had taken services no longer felt able to do so, and therefore the church became lay-led for a time.

In 1974 MCC moved its Sunday services to the Pimlico Neighbourhood Aid Centre, a venue which could be publicly advertised. The large plate-glass frontage meant that services could be observed by anybody walking along Longmoore Street, which may have discouraged some people, but the church thrived nevertheless. During this period MCC London acquired its first full-time pastor, Rev Tom Bigelow, an American and former Episcopalian priest who diligently led the church for some years.

On Tom's return to the USA he was succeeded by Rev Ken Taylor. In 1979, Ken Taylor was succeeded by Rev Jean White, the first woman from the UK to be ordained in UFMCC. That same year she also became the first UK citizen to be elected to the Board of Elders, the governing body of UFMCC.

In 1978–79 the church learnt that the Pimlico Neighbourhood Aid Centre was to be demolished to make way for the Queen Mother Sports Centre. A new home was found at the Cromer Community Centre, in the basement of a block of flats on Argyll Square, near King's Cross station. This was a lot cleaner and tidier than Pimlico, but harder to find!

Friendly Oddfellows

It was felt that the church needed premises that were its own, rather than rented on Sundays. When Jean White suffered a back injury and was confined to bed for a few weeks, she used this time to contact estate agents. As a result she was offered the lease on the upper storey of the two-storey Oddfellows Hall at 2A Sistova Road in Balham. The Oddfellows branch that owned it had suffered a declining membership and decided that they only needed the small ground-floor hall. The church leased the upper floor, consisting of a large hall and small kitchen. This was redecorated and furnished to suit the church's needs.

Having full-time use of this space meant that MCC could use it for weekday meetings, social events and blessing of relationship services. The first service there was held in May 1980.

About this time MCC London attained charity status, the first gay-affirming organisation of any kind to do so. Prior to this all LGBT organisations were deemed to be "political" and therefore not eligible to become a registered charity, so this was a major breakthrough for the LGBT Community.

God's love, we deliver

The South London venue had the drawback that it meant increased travel for some members. For this reason some of its members decided to form MCC North London in 1981. Starting with weekday meetings in an office they soon began holding Sunday services at Marchmont Street in Bloomsbury. Later they secured the use of Bloomsbury Baptist Church and more recently they moved to Trinity United Reformed Church in Camden Town.

One of their members, Hong Tan, was ordained and became their pastor for several years. Their achievements included the founding of God's Love, We Deliver, now known as the Food Chain, in partnership with Oasis North London. This provided meals for people who were incapacitated, especially those with AIDS.

A note from the Editor:

May I just pay tribute to the wonderful work that MCC did in those dark days of the late eighties/early nineties, counselling and helping the bereaved, as well as of course taking a very large number of funeral services. They would sometimes have to take several funeral services within a few weeks. Ed.

Personnel Changes

Rev Hong Tan stood down as pastor when he became the District Co-ordinator for Europe and was replaced by Rev Gill Story and later Rev Pressley Sutherland. Some of the members of MCC North London decided to found MCC in East London. This church, pastored by Rev Jane Clarke, met for some years at St Benet's Chapel in Mile End, but has recently moved to East Ham.

From about 1990 MCC London leased the whole of the building at Sistova Road, Balham. It was able to use the downstairs as a social hall, which further increased its range of events. Central heating was installed and also a chairlift, which were very welcome improvements.

In 1994 Rev Jean White resigned from the pastorate of MCC London in order to take a year's sabbatical. In 1995 she became the founding pastor of MCC South London, which met at a mental health centre in Effra Road, Brixton. There were now four MCCs in London.

A sad farewell

MCC London continued under lay leadership but was unable to find a replacement pastor. Much of the pastor's role was carried out by Michael Moffatt who was training for the clergy. Sadly Michael died of AIDS-related illness in 1997 and the committee decided it was better to close the church and encourage the remaining members to transfer to London's three other churches. Their last service was held in 1998.

Several of the members transferred to MCC South London, which already had a number of former MCC London members in attendance. In 2001 this church took the opportunity to leave the mental health centre in Brixton and move to the United Reformed Church in Balham, about a quarter of a mile from the former meeting place of MCC London in Sistova Road. On 14th June 2009 MCC in East London moved to new premises at Positive East and installed a new pastor, Rev Carmen Margarita Sanchez de Leon, who originally came from Puerto Rico.

The MCC has meanwhile continued to grow in other parts of the UK and worldwide, but a full history is outside the scope of this article.

We are different!

A curiosity of the London (and most European) MCC's is that the services are held in the evenings. At various times morning services have been tried but they have never been popular. The male predominance of the early years has now been rectified and women are well represented. There is also a wide range of ages, ethnicities and Christian traditions represented. Three facts about UFMCC should be mentioned:

1. It is believed to be the largest organisation of any kind in the world with a predominantly LGBT membership.
2. It has the largest proportion of women amongst its clergy of any Christian denomination (now over 50%, with women at the highest levels of the fellowship).
3. It is not an LGBT church; it is an LGBT-affirming church born in the LGBT community, with many straight members.

Contact details for the three churches are as follows:

- MCC East London: e-mail **info@mcceastlondon.org.uk**, website **www.mcceastlondon.org.uk**, Sunday services 5:30 pm at Positive East, 159 Mile End Road, E1 4AD.

- MCC North London: e-mail **welcome@mccnorthlondon.org**, website **www.mccnorthlondon.org**, Sunday services at 7 pm at Trinity URC, corner of Buck Street, Camden Town and Kentish Town Road.

- MCC South London: e-mail **whitesmail@tesco.net**, website **www.mccsouthlondon.co.uk**, PO Box 13242, London SW2 2ZN, Sunday services 6:30 at St Andrew's URC, corner of Laitwood Road and Cavendish Road, Balham, SW12.

Chapter Nineteen
Gay Teachers Group and Schools OUT 1974–

Changing Attitudes?

Rex Batten, who has written a gripping book called "Rid England of This Plague" on his experiences of the 1950s, has some interesting comments on the subject of gay teachers, historically:

The 1967 Act making homosexual relations between two consenting adults legal had very little impact on public opinion. In fact, not all the gay community was in favour. Not long after the Act came in I was talking to a theatrical costumier whom I met when being fitted for a period costume. (Jacket was no problem but the trousers required much more attention!)

There was no doubt about his opinion, "Why did they have to change anything? What was wrong with things as they were? We had our nice little secret, sort of Masonic world. I never went short. Are we expected to go around with a badge saying I'm queer? Life was fun. OK I know there were risks. I ran them but it was part of the excitement. I know what you are going to say. Adults 21. All I can say is I did very nicely, thank you, when I was in my teens. More than one sugar daddy paid for my supper. All these leftie do-gooders are going to spoil everything."

A Secret Society

His attitude was by no means unique and it did reflect the feeling of a large number of gays. There was the feeling of belonging to a tightly knit group and a real fear that it would all be destroyed by coming out. This can be illustrated by the word "Queer". It wasn't used to say we were odd or corrupt. It was a password, secret, masonic, allowing you to enter the world where you could express your natural sexuality.

My experience as a teacher in a boys' school was straightforward homophobia. Coming out, or even letting one's sexuality be known would have cost my job. Why would such a person be working in a boys' school? There could be only one reason. Forty years later that question may still be hinted at.

Yet things have changed. Now the National Union of Teachers has a stall at Gay Pride. In the 1970s strong disapproval was expressed that a teacher in East London had dared let it be known he supported CHE.

When CHE groups were coming into being, teachers could be very homophobic, but there were also signs that things could change. I was told by a member of the PE department that my partner John and I were discussed in the staff room at break time one morning. Were they? Nudge nudge. The investigation was brought to an end by one of the female staff who said, "Well maybe they are—but they've made a better job of their relationship than some of us who I won't name!"

Coming out was almost impossible and made ever worse when Clause 28 came in, and it can still be difficult for an openly gay teacher in a school with boys.[13]

Tony Fenwick of Schools OUT has written the rest of this chapter; we are grateful to him for all the information provided.

First Out of the Closet

The Gay Teachers Group was founded at the University of London Union) in 1974. Life was bleak. Homosexual men were defined in terms of their alleged sexual activities, which had been partially legalised in 1967. That is to say, a maximum of two men could practise same-sex activity in private (ie there must be nobody else in the house)—as long as both were over 21. If one was under 21 he was the victim of a sexual assault and the man over 21 was the assailant—no matter what the circumstances. Lesbians were in a different situation. There was no law governing same sex relationships between women and this was (probably wrongly) attributed to Queen Victoria's alleged refusal to accept that lesbian sex could exist.

Gay men and lesbians were subject to stereotyping. Both were seen as sexual predators but men were effeminate and lesbians were butch. Parodies of gay men by so-called "comedians" such as Dick Emery were a regular feature on Saturday night TV. Many women were perceived as lesbians because they were feminists.

---

[13] Readers are recommended to read Rex's book *Rid England of This Plague* based on his experiences of the 1950s.

In reality many women were challenging patriarchal concepts of femininity. *The Female Eunuch* and *Spare Rib* gave feminism academic status: women were angry and they wanted their identities back. They also wanted equal pay: they were granted it in law in 1975 but in reality women are still fighting for equal pay now—a reminder that the law is a precursor rather than a bringer of change.

The Stonewall riots of 1969 arguably formed the foundations of gay liberation, and CHE was founded in Manchester in that year. London saw its first Pride Rally in 1972. The Gay Teachers Group was one of the groups, together with the Gay Labour Group and Labour Campaign for Gay Rights, that formulated "The Gay Workers' Charter" in late 1974 as a focus for demands to be raised by gays in the Labour movement. Among the unions, NALGO (National Association of Local Government Officers) and NUPE (National Union of Public Employees) had gay groups.

Indeed, the Charter was initially focussed around reformist demands. *Gay News* in 1975 printed five of these demands:

1. equal opportunity of entry into all occupations;
2. equal opportunity in promotion;
3. removal of all laws discriminating against anyone on the grounds of their sexual preferences, particularly in relation to employment and housing.;
4. support for the CHE, Scottish Minorities Group and USFI law reform campaigns;
5. support for the Working Women's Charter.

Not in front of the children

So what was life like for gay and lesbian teachers? It wasn't illegal to be a homosexual teacher; but neither was it illegal to sack a teacher for being homosexual. Nor was it illegal to refuse to employ a teacher for being homosexual.

Both these assertions were proved during that decade, the first in 1974 when John Warburton was sacked for "coming out" to his class. This is what happened, in the words of the then Secretary of the Gay Teachers Group, the late Paul Patrick: "Weeks after the Gay Teachers Group, that eventually became Schools OUT, had been launched in September 1974, I, as its Secretary, received a letter from a supply teacher who had had his contract suspended because, having been seen by pupils on an early Gay Pride March, he affirmed his sexuality when questioned. 1974 was an unforgiving time for lesbian and gay teachers and John Warburton suffered its full force, finding himself between the intransigence of the Inner London Education Authority and the cowardice of the National Union of Teachers."

So there we are. Sacked for coming out to his class by answering a question truthfully—and unsupported by the union whose dues he paid.

As for being refused entrance to the profession, consider the case of Geoff Brighton. Already a successful student at Leeds University, in 1979 Brighton wanted to go on to a teacher training course. He had to take a medical to be cleared for this course and he duly did so. His doctor cleared him as physically fit but found from his medical record that he was homosexual, whereupon he refused him medical clearance and referred him to a psychiatrist.

The general atmosphere of homophobia in the 70s was exacerbated for teachers by the false association with paedophilia. The zeitgeist seemed to be that gay men and lesbians couldn't have children themselves and therefore couldn't have any interest in them unless it was sexual.

All this implies that the Gay Teachers Group was intrinsically political. In reality it was founded as a social group for gay teachers in London, but events pushed it in a political direction. The GTG campaigned on behalf of Warburton and produced a petition demanding his reinstatement. In May 1975 the ILEA rejected it and said the dismissal stood. The campaign was re-launched in 1976 and a book outlining his case was published.

Another founder of the Gay Teachers Group was Sue Sanders. Like John, Sue "outed" herself when a class asked her about her sexual orientation and then went on to discuss it with her class. That should have been the end of the matter; but when a parent wrote to the Head and said she did not want her daughter to be taught by a lesbian, the Head supported the parent and pulled the child from Sue's class. Sue has since taught in Australia and has done a lot of training and counselling. She is currently Co-Chair of Schools OUT and LGBT History Month.

Sue Sanders speaking at the pre-launch of LGBT History Month 2009

To cut a long story short: the Gay Teachers Group campaigned on behalf of Geoff Brighton and he was allowed to undergo training as a teacher. The ILEA's Chief Inspector finally lifted its official prohibition on John Warburton teaching in its borough in 1982—a full eight years after it had sacked him. Throughout the 1970s ILEA was a reactionary thorn in the side of the gay and lesbian teachers' movement. The GTG was banned from advertising in its publications in 1979, and in 1980 it banned the GTG from having meetings on its premises.

Enter Ken Livingstone

All was soon to change. In 1981 left-wing newcomer Ken Livingstone won the Greater London Council elections. He'd committed himself to gay rights in his pre-election campaign and he was keen to deliver. In June of that year, the GTG launched Gay Pride Week. The GLC's Andy Harris came and talked to the group. It was the start of a new process of discussion and accord between the GTG, the GLC and the ILEA. The latter lifted its ban on the GTG using its premises. The aforementioned lifting of the ILEA's ban on Warburton in January 1982 was more than just a personal victory, since the ILEA explicitly recognised the right of teachers to "come out" to pupils in its schools.

In the summer of 1982 the GTG began its monthly social meetings at London Friend. With no Internet and few teachers able to be "out", networking opportunities were virtually non-existent and these meetings were a window of opportunity.

Of course this support from the newly left London ran counter to the national trend. Under the influence of Thatcherism the state was being treated to a good sharp dose of Victorian intolerance. More of that later.

Most teachers are members of a union and they should be able to expect their unions to support them if they have LGBT issues such as evidence of discrimination. This was not always the case. In 1980 the GTG published a pamphlet on the lack of support from the unions. The majority of GTG members were in the National Union of Teachers and there was frustration at its lack of support for lesbians and gays.

In particular, the National Conference, which votes on motions and is therefore the core of the Union's democratic decision-making process, always managed to fudge lesbian and gay rights by talking out a pro-LG motion or by amending it so that it had no effect. This was due to the political manoeuvring of an intransigent executive, who were, to the Union, what the civil service is to government.

Qualified support

Support for gay and lesbian teachers came from the left of the Union, in particular executive member Bernard Regan. He wrote of the 1983 Conference: "The original (gay rights) motion seeks to 'instruct the executive to promote constructive and positive attitudes to gay sexuality in school curricula.' It does not say schools have to adopt these positions. The Executive amendment ... calls for Conference to re-affirm 'its support for the union's consistent stand against discrimination on the grounds of gender, marital status, ethnic origin, religious or political belief and sexual orientation.'

"However, the amendment continued: 'Conference also re-affirms its belief that the content and development of the curriculum of the school is a matter for the individual school concerned, and repudiates any attempt by outside intervention to impose curricular restraints upon the school'.

'Whilst therefore the amendment has an apparently liberal position on Gay Rights the second part of it reflects the kind of prejudice that sees homosexual teachers as proselytising amongst their students! It is a contradictory position which gives with the one hand and takes away with the other. It is time for a change'."

Jersey!

Another feature of the 1983 NUT Conference was more significant. It was held in Jersey. While this might have been a treat for straight delegates, it criminalised the gay male ones, since male homosexuality was still illegal on the island. The Gay Teachers Group raised its objections—and the Union solicitor advised them not to engage in any homosexual activity at the Conference!

It was a fractious conference which began with gay campaigner Peter Bradley being sent from the rostrum for not speaking on the motion before he could complete his first sentence. Tim Lucas gave a resounding speech conveying his anger that his own Union had criminalised him by sending him to a conference in Jersey. It ended with a Socialist Teachers' Association Disco where people danced with partners of their own sex! The important point, however, was that the GTG managed to raise the profile of lesbian and gay teachers at this event, and that the mindset of the NUT was changed for good.

The Inner London Education Authority and the Greater London Council developed their radical agenda, and things grew apace during the early eighties. The ILEA created a "Gay Working Party" with the GTG, the Gay Youth Movement and others, which was to advise and inform on recruitment and retention and on curriculum development. The Women's committee of the GLC set up a Lesbian Working Party, also giving grants to applicants from the LGB community—such as London Lesbian and Gay Switchboard.

Dark days and Section 28

Then, in the mid-eighties, AIDS wreaked havoc among the gay community. Its tragic effects were bad enough in themselves, but the media hysteria around "the gay plague" exacerbated the pain and suffering inflicted on people and the loved ones they lost. Gay teachers were ostracised by their colleagues, some of whom refused to use the same toilets or share mugs— and in 1985 the GTG was moved to produce guidance busting the myths circulating about HIV and AIDS.

Thatcher got rid of the GLC in 1986. She regarded it as an abomination and now it was a case of one down, one to go. The ILEA and its progressive agenda was the next target. Riding on the wave of hysteria over the AIDS pandemic, the *Daily Express* and the *Daily Mail* found something to incense the public: *Cathy Lives with Eric and Martin*. A Danish book originally, the text was translated into English and it told the story of a little girl with two dads. The right-wing press made a tremendous fuss about this book being put into schools, and it was the fall-out from the outrage that led to the dreadful Section 28 and ultimately sounded the death-knell for the ILEA in 1990.

Section 28, however, united the opposition if nothing else. Now there was a cause for all to fight against! It led to the foundation of Stonewall in the UK, and the teaching unions were united in their condemnation of the "Clause". With so many activists around, the GTG had to re-think its role. First, it was a social organisation with affiliated branches in the north east, the north west, Birmingham, Leicester, Nottingham, Bristol, Wales, and of course London. Secondly it provided a telephone service or point of contact. This was not an advice or counselling service so much as a means of pointing LGB teachers in the right direction if they needed counselling or advice.

These were dark days for GTG. The abolition of the ILEA and the GLC, together with the arrival of Section 28, caused a feeling of helplessness to ripple through the Group. In the early days it played a role in advising the "new kids on the block": Stonewall. This was a movement of actors and media types, such as Sir Ian McKellen, Michael Cashman and Simon Fanshawe, who had been relatively apolitical but were appalled by this Act. GTG liaised with them at the Drill Hall and gave them a grounding in activism in general and what it was like at the chalkface in particular.

The advantage of Stonewall was that it included a number of media people who knew how to button-hole the press, as well as actors and celebrities who could give the cause glamour and popularise it.

Schools OUT is born

Nevertheless the GTG, if it were to survive in difficult times, needed to rethink its role. Firstly its members re-named it Schools OUT, after its last publication in 1987. Then they adopted an inclusive approach and added to the lesbian and gay categories the words "bisexual" and "transsexual". This was not unanimously popular and some older members left in disgust at such groups being attached. However, like most of its initiatives, Schools OUT found itself ahead of its time. It developed a new constitution with cross-union affiliations and rules.

When I joined in May 1995 the age of consent for homosexual men had been reduced to 18, after a bitter night in the Commons. I became male contact after an AGM in Birmingham where I met the team. This meant I had my telephone number in *Gay Times* and people rang when they had some problems. The overwhelming number of problems for gay male teachers concerned indecency offences and particularly cottaging.

Teachers are bound by law to reveal all criminal offences, because a condition of being cleared to teach is that no offences can be "spent". Thus I have to reveal that I was prosecuted for driving with a defective tyre in 1983, every single year! Teachers who were newly qualified had to declare convictions for sexual offences when applying for posts, and this was always a cause of fear and trepidation.

Nor was this without good reason. An offence committed by a 19-year-old in 1992 was still an offence after 1994. As it was, there were two pieces of casework involving teachers whose offer of a placement was retracted when it was found out that they'd been caught in a sexual act in their teens! It was an early experience for me of how stupid the law could be and how vindictive institutional homophobia can be.

Unions provided better representation then. Our Chair John Burns was a regional officer for the NUT and he was on hand to give sound advice. My female equivalent was Sue Sanders and she had more cases of discrimination at work. Steve Bonham was treasurer and a member of the NASUWT. At last we had the unions on board!

A serious setback

One case that was never resolved successfully was that of Shirley Pearce. A successful science teacher until she was found to be a lesbian, Pearce endured horrific homophobic bullying from the pupils at her school. The Head didn't support her—using the "You brought it on yourself" line. She was defended by the NASUWT and the NUT and by Schools OUT but ultimately every case and every tribunal was lost. There was no question that she had endured horrid abuse and had been abandoned by her irresponsible employers. But there was no law against it. The Sex Discrimination Act was deemed only to deal with gender; not sexual orientation.

When the case reached the High Court it was defeated by an expensive lawyer called Cherie Blair! To this day Shirley Pearce has not been given justice.

Then LAGER, the lesbian and gay legal advice service that we relied upon for our best information, lost its funding and was closed down.

By the mid-nineties Schools OUT was less important than it had been as a national organisation, but local affiliated groups were up and running. However, the internet took over the socialising role and by the early nineties the local groups had all but fizzled out.

New Labour

Expectations of New Labour after 1997 were high. Things didn't change overnight, but the combination of a government generally committed to equality and European legislation that moved us on meant that a lot of the changes we'd been fighting for (in some cases all our lives) were coming about. The pivotal year was 2003, when Section 28 was scrapped and it became illegal to discriminate against lesbian and gay people in the workplace.

Schools OUT was still disappointed, however, at the slow pace of change in our schools. Management teams still seemed to behave as though Section 28 remained in place. One explanation could be found in the fear of how parents might react. Another, especially under a Labour administration, was fear of the right-wing press. But following the murder of Stephen Lawrence and the outcome of the inquiry in 1999, there was a change in public sector institutions. The term "institutional racism" made people think about racism as a phenomenon that was endemic within an organisation rather than a combined effect of individual bigotries. And institutional racism turned into institutional sexism, "disableism" and homophobia.

This was something the Metropolitan Police were made acutely aware of, and there was a consequential attitudinal sea-change. Sue Sanders of Schools OUT did awareness training for the Met and has since done so for a host of other police authorities and public bodies. But schools were still resistant to awareness training.

Meanwhile homophobic—and transphobic—bullying continued unabated. If anything, things were getting worse, especially with the ubiquitous use of the term "gay" used within youth culture to signify "dysfunctional".

LGBT History Month begins

The new co-chairs of Schools OUT were Sue Sanders and Paul Patrick, and they began to see that another barrier to progress within our school communities was that LGBT people were seen as victims. Bullied, beaten, murdered, at risk of HIV infection and AIDS, what little education there was about us objectified us as pathetic in the true sense of the word; to be pitied rather than given true equality.

This in turn perpetuated a notion that you were better off straight—and thence a notion that it was OK to run the gauntlet of taunts and abuse at school if accused of being gay or lesbian, as though it were a challenge to be overcome. In turn, Sue's work with the Police, and then the criminal justice system and the Probation Service, showed that homophobia and transphobia had enormous social and financial costs in the adult world, and this increased her determination to try to conquer it in schools.

Paul Patrick at Pride London 2007

Then the idea emerged. There was a Black History Month in the UK. There was a GLBT History Month in the US. Why not have a Rainbow History Month? Following a question put by myself to the then Equalities Department's Minister for Women, Jacqui Smith, at the TUC Lesbian and Gay Conference in 2004, at which she expressed the Government's support, LGBT History Month was born on a wing and a prayer. The idea was to claim our rightful place in history and provide positive role models in the form of successful lesbians, gay men, bisexuals and trans people who had made great achievements in their time. Further, we wanted to assert

OUT OF THE SHADOWS

that LGBT people, by many other names, had existed in all times and all places.

The first such event was held in February 2005. It is now the biggest event in the UK LGBT calendar, with thousands of events to celebrate it every year and a ringing endorsement from Gordon Brown in the form of a Downing Street Reception in 2009 and from London Mayor Boris Johnson.[14]

In 2007, Schools OUT supported Claire Anderson of the NUS in producing the biggest petition in the world. Made up of a barely finite number of sheets loosely sewn together, with painted footprints from a huge number of people gathered at a host of Pride events throughout the summer of that year, the 270 foot long petition was taken to the Department for Education and Science and presented to Education Minister Jacqui Smith. The video can still be seen on You-Tube.[15]

In 2008, Schools OUT launched an on-line tool-kit for LGBT students, made by students, with FAQs and support.[16]

In 2009 our treasurer David Watkins launched A Day in Hand, an international campaign to get same sex people holding hands in public. Its world-wide popularity can be seen in the tapestry of photographs that have already been gathered on the website.[17]

Much achieved and much still to do

These events boosted the popularity and influence of Schools OUT enormously. Attendance at our annual conference increased from 17 in 2004 to 135 in 2005. We have been in the offices of the DfES, the DCSF, OFSTED and the GTC. We are consulted on documents and Government legislation. We are now a web-based organisation that supports teachers, pupils, students, parents, heads, governors, TAs, dinner staff and janitorial staff, in the quest to make our schools safe spaces for LGBT people.

---

[14] www.lgbthistorymonth.org.uk

[15] www.youtube.com/watch?v=_N2BEdyUQQo

[16] www.schools-out.uk/STK

[17] www.adayinhand.com

Dan Snow made a big fuss of Hadrian's love for Antinous in his biography, and Antinous' bust is now in its rightful place in the British Museum; next to the Emperor. Sue Perkins, John Barrowman and Stephen K Amos are on our TV screens instead of Dick Emery. But we still have to eradicate homophobia and transphobia in our schools.

We remember fondly: John Burns, who was National Secretary of Schools OUT during the 1990s and died after a short illness on April 1st, 2001; and Paul Patrick, who helped found the organisation in 1974 and was, as far as we are aware, Britain's first openly gay teacher. He was still co-chair when he died on May 22nd, 2008. Paul's obituary can be found online.[18]

Tim Lucas retired after serving on the Schools OUT committee for over 20 years and being its treasurer until 2007. He now has honorary membership. Steve Bonham left in 2002 to join the human wall against the occupation in Palestine. He is now back in the UK and continues to support the Palestinian peoples.

Further reading:

The Gay Workers' Charter, a critical history of a UK gay union activists' group, by John Witte.

Open and Positive, by John Warburton. GTG.

Gay Rights and the Teaching Trade Unions. GTG.

---

[18] www.lgbthistorymonth.org.uk/history/paulpatrick.htm

Chapter Twenty
The Transport Group 1974–

by Malcolm Malins

Beginnings

Back in November 1973 the following small ad appeared in *Gay News* Number 35. "Transport Enthusiasts. rail, bus, tram. Want to form a gay transport group? Or meet gays with same interest? Box 35/46"

This was the start of the Gay Transport Group with its first meeting early in 1974 in a North London flat. Beginning with around 12 to 15 members and continuing to this day with currently around 90, the group celebrated 35 years of existence in 2009. A contact ad for the group continued to be published in *Gay News* and then in *Gay Times* under the social groups listings "special interests" until that most useful source of information was discontinued.

It was decided in those early days that we would hold slide or film shows related to transport mainly in the winter months with visits to places of transport interest when the better summer weather could be enjoyed. All this would be co-ordinated by the group's founder, Ken Glazier, who had placed that ad in *Gay News* back in 1973, with reliance on the membership to host the meetings in their homes, present the shows and organise the trips. There never was a committee, so the hassle of committee meetings, minutes, AGMs etc. has always been avoided.

Until March 2007, when sadly and most unexpectedly, Ken Glazier died, he had carried the burden of administration and running the group single-handed, with only the copying and distribution of the monthly newsletter/programme done by another member. This was not an arduous task for him as the membership continually produced the material for programmes, arranged the excursions and provided the meeting places enabling him to produce the diary of events over the coming year. We still do not have a formal committee. The membership of the group has always been concentrated in London and Home Counties but has members from all over the country.

Special Events

Early on at least three meetings were held on BBC premises, at TV Centre and Lime Grove studios, where those attending found themselves taking tea in one of the staff canteens with the cast of *Blakes 7* and the likes of Michael Fish and Wendy Craig. Despite such a wide scattering of members across the country, many have attended the London meetings on a surprisingly regular basis and have made a valuable contribution to the continuing success of the group. Conversely, on trips out from the London area to places such as the West Country, Wales or the North, we have been able to meet up with local members on their home territory. We met our Belfast member on one such trip whilst he was holidaying in Blackpool.

The content of the winter meetings have varied enormously over the years as too, dare I say it, at times has the quality. The group has been fortunate in having a number of members with a great wealth of experience, some from a professional standpoint within the industry and some as enthusiastic amateurs. Some are published authors on the subject like the late Ken Glazier, our founder, with many books on London Buses to his credit. Many have extensive archives of photographs, slides and publications to draw upon. Others are or were involved in filming the industry as semi-professionals or as gifted amateurs. Yet more have skills as presenters, all of which has led to the vast range of subjects covered in the slide and film shows which the group has enjoyed over the years. There has been an occasional speaker from outside the group as well.

There has also been a regular photographic competition judged by the members (the first one was judged by the then staff photographer from *Gay News*, Bob Workman). A members' slide evening is usually held each year enabling members who would be unable to fill a whole evening on one subject to show up to 20 slides on any aspect of transport.

Red Rovers and Round Robins

In the early days there were trips out around London using the Red Rover tickets which were restricted to bus travel. In more recent years these became known as "Travelcard bashes" and would also feature travel by tube and train as the flexibility of such tickets permits this. Members of a certain age enjoy free travel within the Capital so this becomes a great free day out for them, in the company of other like-minded souls.

A development of this, from 2000, has been a treasure hunt. A couple of members have got together and written out clues for the others to solve, requiring visits to various locations within the capital making use of the Travelcard or passes. The participants go off usually in groups of two or three to solve the clues. There are prizes to be won and a substantial buffet to be enjoyed at a member's home at the end.

During the 1970s and into the 80s British Rail operated a programme of excursions, usually by scheduled services, under the titles of "Merrymakers" or "Round Robins" at very acceptable prices to a multitude of places across the UK, including locations featuring preserved railways or transport museums, or somewhere like Blackpool for the trams. There were also private operators who ran chartered excursion trains aimed at transport enthusiasts (including the straight variety), covering extensive mileage and often obscure routes to appropriate venues.

Costs have risen considerably since those early days but the group has continued to venture out on trips to centres of preservation on service trains from London, on one occasion taking a day trip to Brussels by Eurostar for lunch. Additionally some of the group members have had "contacts" and could arrange rides on historic and preserved vehicles, for example on the London to Brighton Historic Vehicle run, which would not normally be open to the general public.

The canal trip from Little Venice, near Paddington

More recently the group has cruised the Regents Canal from Little Venice, both westwards to Brentford Docks and eastwards to Regents Canal Dock in Limehouse.

The group also cruised part of the Grand Union Canal in Hertfordshire whilst partaking of a strawberry cream tea—very genteel.

The group's activities benefit from having many members with professional backgrounds within the transport industry and others much involved with the preservation of historic vehicles, some being vehicle owners themselves. This has resulted in the chance for members to visit places like Fulwell bus depot, Southend bus garage, Delaines at Bourne and such obscure historic locations as the old City and South London Railway tube tunnels under the Thames by London Bridge, the Post Office tube railway at Mount Pleasant, and more modern ones such as an underground tour of North Greenwich Station on the Jubilee line extension before it opened; we even took part in an evacuation exercise from a "crashed" train in the tunnels under the river prior to the line opening.

Trips were made "overseas" to the Isle of Man and the Isle of Wight! Not quite overseas, but definitely on the seas, were trips on the paddle steamer *Lincoln Castle* on the Humber, and twice on PS *Waverley* down the Thames to Southend in 1984 and 2005. On the 1984 cruise "ancient" (ie our 1947-built *Waverley*) met "modern" when the new hydrofoil service between Ostend and London passed us at speed causing so many of our passengers to gather on the port side of *Waverley* that the starboard paddle came out of the water and provoked a hurried request over the public address system from the Captain for us to move back, as he could not steer the vessel with us all on one side! There was another cruise on *Waverley* along the South coast from Newhaven to Hastings; on this trip we were approached by a couple of the crew members asking where the best gay bars were in Brighton as they fancied a night out. Those were the days when wearing a Lambda badge was a means of identifying yourself as gay and some of the lads from Glasgow in the crew recognised ours!

Going Abroad

It was not until March 1995 that the group ventured overseas to foreign parts, to Brussels and Ghent following the opening of the Channel Tunnel in November 1994. Since that date there have been annual visits into Europe; twice to France, three times to Switzerland, four visits to Germany, once each to Austria and the Netherlands and once to Italy. 2008 saw us return to Belgium, this time based in Antwerp, and the 2009 trip was to Vienna. We travel, when practicable, all the way by train, starting with Eurostar from London, but it has been more sensible to fly to some destinations.

Going all the way by train to Berlin, Dresden and also Zurich were not bad achievements. Whilst on these trips the members have often enjoyed private tram charters such as in Antwerp.

We also had private tram charters to Heidelberg and Innsbruck, the dining tram tour in Basel and a private hire of the dining train, on a line out of Lausanne, plus the rack railways near Lucerne (with a private car attached to the service train up the Rigi), the paddle steamers on the lakes, and guided tours of tram depots in Milan, Basel, St Etienne and Innsbruck.

Malcolm in front of a tram in Antwerp, during a group trip

Perhaps the group's most exciting highlight on these trips was when we visited a preserved steam line in Germany only a few miles from our base in Basel. Having chatted up some of the volunteers whilst on the outbound steam trip we were given a tour of the steam sheds at the end of the line at Kandoren. To our surprise they then invited us all to join a brake van trip behind their steam loco on the mainline all the way back into Basel. It was a training run for one of their drivers, a lady, and we ran wrong line all the way for quite some distance. We were so glad there was nothing scheduled to be coming the other way on our line!

The most ambitious overseas trip took place in 2000 when eight members flew to California via Phoenix and spent two weeks travelling from San Diego in the south (with a side trip down to Mexico using the "Tijuana Trolley"), to San Francisco and Sacramento in the North. All travel was by train, bus, tram and light rail, and that in a country not famed for its public transport links. The light rail lines in San Jose, Sacramento and San Diego were explored plus streetcar and trolleybus networks in San Francisco.

There was one exception to all this public transport. In order to visit a remotely located trolley museum at Rio Vista Junction east of San Francisco, hire cars were needed for the 100 mile or so round trip. The highlight of the stay was a private tram charter around much of the system in San Francisco—not on just any old tram but the open, single deck Blackpool "boat car" in their historic collection.

Fame at Last

The group has also featured in the media (with an article in *Gay News*), been interviewed by a Dutch gay organisation for a local Dutch radio programme, and in 1997 found ourselves in front of a Dutch TV news crew on Amsterdam Centraal station as we got off a train. True, on that occasion we were not being interviewed as the Transport Group; they just happened to catch two of us and were asking about our feelings on the election results. It was May 1997 and the day after a certain Mr Blair came to power.

The Dutch radio team were in the UK, just London I suspect, gathering material about the developing network of gay clubs, societies and presumably the commercial scene as well, during the 1970s. At that time The Netherlands were somewhat more open and advanced compared with the UK, Dutch law being more relaxed towards gay lifestyles than the UK. Quite how they came to choose the Transport Group is not known but three members met up with them in their hotel room near Marble Arch, where they were treated to coffee and cakes and asked a few questions about the aims and objectives of the group.

More significant was the interview which took place at the offices of *Gay News* in 1976. A series of articles were appearing about the various gay social groups that were springing up in the capital and across the country, and the group was invited to take part. Again, it was three members who found themselves in front of the then features editor, Keith Howes, answering questions and explaining the purpose of the group and how it was developing, and giving personal histories.

The finished article together with a photo of members on a trip to the Bluebell Railway (at the start of the chapter) subsequently appeared in *Gay News* issue 108 and led to a healthy increase in membership numbers. It also led to a work colleague of one of the three coming out to him after reading it. The founder of the group is fourth from right and the author of this piece, second from right.

The Social Side

There is also a social side to the activities of the group. There are plenty of opportunities for members to chat and socialise over refreshments which are an integral part of the regular meetings and also at group dinners. In more recent years members have got together for an evening meal at various restaurants in London, usually around Easter time. In July there is a garden party, currently held each year in Brighton often with over 30 members attending, some with their partners. Fortunately, this has nearly always been blessed with sunny weather. With around a third of the membership present it is also the nearest we come to an AGM as it is the time when the programme and timetable for the following twelve months is planned and discussed—but only after feasting on a substantial buffet.

That original ad brought together many gay transport enthusiasts over the years, a significant number of whom have been in the group for most of its 35 years of existence. Long-standing friendships have been formed, and in a few cases have become partnerships. Inevitably, over time, we have lost a number of friends too. Members who were in their 20s or 30s when the group started are now somewhat more mature in age but remain active and enthusiastic in their support and together with, hopefully, new recruits, will see the Transport Group continue for many more years to come.

Malcolm Malins[19]

---

[19]   Malcolm is a founder member and current Chairman of the Transport Group. We are very grateful to him for providing us with all the information both for this chapter and for the chapter on the Marypad group.

Chapter Twenty-One
Bexley and Bromley Gay Groups 1974–2001

It has been rather difficult to find out about the Bromley CHE group which started in the 1970s. We do know that if more or less closed down at one point, and had a short-lived revival when Ross Burgess was area "Field Officer" for CHE and found a potential volunteer to act as Convenor.

Most of the information about Bromley is really about activities which the very successful Magnet group, based in Bexley, started there quite a bit later in the 1980s.

One of the few references we have found to activities actually run by the early Bromley group is that of a disco held in Catford—quite a long way from Bromley town.

Things were, however, much more locally based in the neighbouring Borough of Bexley. We now give you some extracts from the Badgers/Magnet history:

From Badgers to Magnet

by Paul Knight

Magnet was the more recent guise of a group formed back in the "closet" days of 1974 by Bexley Campaign for Homosexual Equality—Bexley CHE. From the humble beginnings, as they say, of 20 interested members at the original meeting, to the heady days of Badgers in 1981 when membership ran to over 400. Bexley And Dartford Gay Educational Recreational Society began to metamorphose at The Woodman at Blackfen, Kent.

The objection to CHE being at The Woodman was in no small way due to the announcement in the local paper that the venue was being used by a gay group. Under pressure from his regular customers, the unfortunate landlord of the pub, although sympathetic, could do no more than protect his own image and that of the pub, so had to cancel the arrangement. However he did manage to allow us the use of the room when the fuss had died down. It was then decided to stop sending out newsletters to outside bodies, and work more "undercover".

Action was taken to contact Bexley Council (also Kent and Bromley councils) regarding the discrimination against gay teachers, and to ask the Education Committee if they were prepared to give time to speakers from the Group to speak to 16–18 year old boys and girls in local schools on Homosexuality.

CHE was a fighting force, but the need for social intercourse was the catalyst for Badgers to arise, helping gays to come to terms with their own life style and to gain the courage to participate in a more "public" life with visits to other members' homes, pubs and clubs.

In 1986 the group put on a very successful revue called *Cinderfella* in a basement somewhere in Bexley, and we are pleased to show you a photo of this famous occasion.

Cinderfella in a **Bexley basement, 1986**

In the mid-eighties Magnet started to hold regular social evenings at the delightful Swan & Mitre in Bromley (inevitable jokes about S & M evenings!) which strengthened the links between the two towns as far as gays were concerned. There were particularly pleasant evenings in the summer when the walled garden at the back of the pub could be used, and the management was always friendly. Although there was still an underlying suspicion, there was by this time also a general acceptance and no longer such a stigma to being gay. In this more relaxed atmosphere, the nature of social groups changed.

The Swan and Mitre pub in Upper Bromley High Street

Badgers changed again to Magnet, with the accent on a social level of like lifestyles. We had a healthy programme of visits to members' homes, pubs, and clubs, and friendly rivalry of quizzes and competitions.

A note from the Editor:

I met Paul Knight and David Percy for lunch in January 2010—oddly enough at the Swan & Mitre in Bromley—when they very kindly gave me most of the material in this chapter. I was sad to learn, only a month after our lunch meeting, that Paul had passed away. We are very glad to have been able to include his thoughts and memories in the book.

How Magnet drew people in

by David Percy

Sidcup can lay claim to having the most popular public venue used by Magnet. Champers was a small wine bar, which was later renamed Bar Sastre. The new Spanish owner and his English wife welcomed us whole-heartedly and we took them to our hearts—fairy lights around the bar, a heady mix of Abba and Gipsy Kings, and often open past closing time— what was there not to like? To top it all, given his love of Abba, the owner's name was Fernando.

We used to meet once a month informally at Bar Sastre, with Bromley's Swan & Mitre and Mendelssohn's Wine Bar alternating on the other two weeks each month. (The latter two were a few doors away from each other in Upper Bromley High Street).

I think Fernando's sincerity was proved one evening when I had to break to him the unfortunate news that one of our members, a regular visitor to the Bar Sastre, had been killed in a road accident. Later that evening I came across Fernando hiding round the back of the bar crying profusely, so upset was he by the news. Unfortunately financial problems forced them to close for business in September 1995.

The member killed in the accident was Philip Cook, and we honoured his memory with an annual award given by vote to one of Magnet's members in recognition of their services to the group or to the wider gay community. (Dave Latchem was the recipient in 1994).

Meetings at the Swan & Mitre had stopped in 1991. It was November 1995 before we were back in Bromley again on a regular basis when we were looking for somewhere to fill the void created by the loss of our Sidcup venue. We found a Belgian bar called Abbaye, situated off Queen's Gardens next to The Glades, Bromley's shopping precinct. Abbaye proved very popular with members until a change of management in late 1998, so in February 1999 we moved to Henry's Café Bar in Ringers Road, just off the High Street. This was a fairly noisy venue (all hard surfaces, no soft furnishings) but popular enough with most who used it. However some members were put off attending because of reports in the press citing the bar as a haunt of the gang accused of the murder of

Stephen Lawrence. Our time there was relatively short-lived since in October 1999 we were on the move again.

Indeed, October 1999 was a momentous month for Bromley-based gays because this month saw the opening of the area's first ever gay pub, the Crown and Anchor.

This pub, situated close to Bromley North rail station, thus became our new Bromley venue with regular fortnightly visits until July 2000 and occasional visits thereafter—until the group went the way of Monty Python's famous Norwegian Blue parrot.

Greenwich

Our first foray into Greenwich, at least during my time, was in February 1991 to The Gloucester in King William Walk, opposite one of the entrances to Greenwich Park. Newly opened under gay management the previous year, this pub was very touristy during the day, very gay in the evening. It was popular with many of our members and the group continued to use it until March 1995, when members could no longer tolerate the loud level of the pub music.

So we switched our allegiance to another gay (or at least gay/straight mixed) pub—the rather cosier and considerably quieter Ye Olde Rose and Crown situated next to Greenwich Theatre in Crooms Hill, continuing with regular visits until the very end. Also of mention is the Lone Sailor, a gay pub situated the other (and some would say downmarket) side of the Cutty Sark—an even quieter but very friendly pub, with a great welcome from Belle its landlady. We made use of the pub's function room for various Magnet special events (e.g. in 1994 we held three events there: two parties including one at Christmas and a safe-sex discussion led by a visiting outreach worker).

Magnet moves closer to Central London

Following the cessation of our regular visits to Bromley's Crown and Anchor, we searched for a new venue within easy reach of the majority of members and in August 2000 settled upon the Watch House, a Wetherspoon pub in Lewisham—finally, a pub without music! And, of course, it offered reasonably priced drinks.

We saw good attendances initially but, by the time the group was approaching its final days, we were lucky to find more than half a dozen of us gathered together, both there and at Ye Olde Rose and Crown.

In February 1994 we started meeting up every six weeks at the well-known Halfway to Heaven. This was intended as an early evening gathering for those working in central London and the turnout was usually fairly high—and as a place to meet you couldn't get much more central than this—also very convenient for Charing Cross.

We continued to meet there until November 1996 when we moved to the nearby and equally gay Paradise Bar in George Court, just off the south side of The Strand. By the time we dropped this place as a regular venue in January 1998 it had been through two name changes: first Popstarz Bar and then the Retro Bar.

Disco dancing

Apart from the regular and not-so-regular visits to various pubs and bars, we also made the occasional trip to a club or disco—indeed, until the spring of 1990 we held our own monthly disco. Like most other social groups, we also participated in many other events such as meals out, trips to the theatre, weekends away and holidays abroad—and throughout Magnet's existence many members opened up their homes for coffee evenings, film nights, parties and so forth.

Magnet membership was mainly spread across the four London boroughs of Bexley, Bromley, Lewisham and Greenwich but some of our members lived farther afield, particularly towards the Medway towns. Of course, we did have the odd member living north of the river, even one who lived in the north of England! We didn't see him too often.

Perhaps longer than most groups, Magnet continued to have monthly discos right into the early nineties. One venue was the social club attached to the New Eltham Football Club. Then, coincidentally we tried a few discos, believe it or not, at the Charlton Football Club, which were very popular and only stopped as our contact there retired. In its heyday our discos attracted 100. Later we used to attend the "Magic" discos in Gillingham at an establishment named Ritzy's, organised by our parallel group, Magic, a bit further out into Kent, covering the Medway area.

Last days of Magnet

When did Magnet end? The group's effective demise was in October 2001. October was when we held our AGM and elected a new committee but on this occasion only two people had put themselves forward for election. Apart from the poor attendance at events generally, the Magnet membership numbers had been in decline for two or three years and in 2001 had fallen to a record low. It was time to consider seriously whether the group had any future; nevertheless, it was decided that Magnet should try to continue in some capacity. But within a couple of months it was fairly obvious that this was not going to work and a proposal to formally disband the group was unanimously accepted at an Extraordinary General Meeting in January 2002.

Nevertheless, it is comforting to know that one popular Magnet activity survives to this day—ten pin bowling. A small crowd of ex-Magneteers still go to the Lewisham bowling alley every month or two.

Late developments in Bromley

In Bromley, the Bromley Gay and Bisexual Men's Group (which meets in Anerley) has been around for nearly ten years, but we are not sure whether SNAP still exists. SNAP (Sexuality Not A Problem!) was a group for young gay men, lesbians and bisexuals, under 25, living in or around Bromley.

Sadly both of Bromley's gay pubs—the Crown & Anchor and then the Star & Garter—have both gone under, the latter very recently.

However, you will be pleased to know that Bromley-town gays finally asserted themselves on 30th July 2005 when a Gay Pride rally was held in the streets to protest at the local council refusing to recognise gay civil partnerships. We have much pleasure in including some photographs from the day on the next page.

Laurie Smith records that the March was a success—well over 100 people turned out in a small corner of SE London to mark their disapproval—over 2000 people signed the petition to say they objected to the council's position. In fact people were coming up and signing the petition as the march was passing. Well done, Bromley gays! (And by the way, Bromley council later relented).

Gay Pride in Bromley town, 2005

Chapter Twenty-Two
CHE Youth Group 1974–c.1980

by Ian Mair

The Background

London, June 1974. I arrived in a drab capital city, World War Two bomb sites still gaping, buildings black with years of soot and grime. The "swinging sixties" had well and truly run their course, and all had returned to a banal normality. London shut at 11 pm, except for Sundays when it was 10:30, so that you could get to the nine-to-five job without a hangover. During the week, people scampered on and off crowded commuter trains during the rush hours to travel to and from dull 60s offices to even duller 70s homes in the middle of nowhere. There were strikes, recessions, and if that was not grim enough, three governments—Heath, Wilson, Callaghan—all teetered on the brink of deserved oblivion.

But the evenings provided relief from the grind of daily life. Even at that time, there was a terrific amount happening on the gay scene. Apart from the pubs—Imperial in Richmond, Champion in Notting Hill, Salisbury in St Martin's Lane, Black Cap in Camden, Father Redcap and Union in Camberwell, Vauxhall, William IV in Hampstead, Wheatsheaf in Goldhawk Road. There were also clubs, some highly respectable but some with slightly dodgy reputations—Shanes, the Sombrero, Gigolo, Catacombs, Masquerade, Napoleon's (sugar daddy land) and various others which came and went such as Chaguarama's. Even one of my now local pubs, the Wheatsheaf at Tooting Bec, had a gay night for a while run by WAGS. Then a couple of big clubs opened to great effect—Bang disco, which became G-A-Y (the Astoria in Tottenham Court Road—being demolished for Crossrail as I write) and Heaven. There were legendary drag balls at the Porchester Hall (ended by the delightful Shirley Porter—budget cuts or homophobia?).

And the dress of those days—completely tasteless, but fun. Whereas the sixties had shown great style, the seventies took things to excess—wide lapels, flared or baggy trousers, floral shirts with round collars, kipper ties, platform shoes. So you got togged up and went out to the venues, revelling in that delightful feeling of doing something somewhat illicit!

Taking Shape

But there was more available. A friend who had arrived in London a long time before I did invited me to meet one of his friends who was membership secretary of the CHE London Youth Group. I can remember him, but not his name—but the phrase "Dollis Hill", near Willesden, comes to mind. He gave me some details.

The Group had been started by some existing young CHE members who wanted to provide a way for other young gays to come out, in a less stressful and exploitative atmosphere than the commercial gay scene which was expensive, rather intimidating (can you remember your first visit to a gay pub?), and lacked the potential for making friends with people (yes, OK and shagging—many thanks to Denis Potter's *Singing Detective* series for bringing that word back into use), so they set up the CHE Youth Group for people, of both (all?) sexes under twenty-five.

By an amazing coincidence, I have the newsletters which were published during my time as a member of the group. I was struck by the sheer number of events—at least one every week. I also observed the correctness of the grammar and accuracy of the punctuation!

So excitedly I went on Tuesday evening of the 4th June 1974 to the CHE London Information Centre at 22 Great Windmill Street. I looked with curious disdain at the hotbed of heterosexual exploitation, the Windmill Theatre—something else that has changed its reputation from being an outcast from decent society to a national treasure. Looking back at the newsletter, the talk was about the functions of CHELIC itself, but more interesting was actually meeting several of the regular members.

The location of the meeting was unusual, in that it was on CHE premises. Normally the meetings were held either in members' homes, or in the homes of people who were supportive of the group, but were too old to be members. In the sixties it was relatively easy to get a flat in central London, and people with those flats could hang onto them, as they tended to be controlled tenants. It was only in the seventies that it became virtually impossible to find a flat in Greater London, let alone the centre. The use of people's homes allowed a more informal atmosphere during meetings, and I suppose for this reason the Group developed differently from most of the other groups which had central meeting points. There were at least eight different locations in inner London, but there were also outer London destinations such as Shepherds Bush, Battersea, Clapham/Balham, Maida Vale, Putney, Manor House and as far out as Brentford (of which more later).

Although total membership peaked at about 70 people, fewer attended meetings. Typically attendance was in the teens for a talk, so could be fitted into a reasonable sized reception room. I remember sitting on the floor on several occasions. Parties were more popular, peaking at 80.

A Time of Liberation

Meetings were arranged with a great deal of effort from the enthusiastic committee members. Meetings, usually held first and third Tuesdays of the month, consisted usually of a speaker on a topic of interest held at members' or friends' homes. Each month there was also an entertainment visit to the theatre or opera, a party or two organised by members and a visit to a disco or some other events. For a period, Wednesdays were tried and sometimes there were meetings weekly.

The topics covered in talks were many and varied. Favourite areas were: the workings of CHE (although this subject sounds excruciating now, I don't remember any of the talks being boring); sex (surprisingly enough); health (usually about VD); beauty (we must have been a real bunch of narcissists); gay lifestyles (editors of magazines, photographers—how we did preen ourselves when they were around); counselling (various).

June 1974 must have been a vintage month, as there were three speakers—one on CHELIC mentioned already, another on Transsexual Liberation and the third on Brixton Gay Liberation. At the time, Gay Liberation or GLF was very big and active—they were left-wing politically and favoured areas such as Brixton, which I believe was one of their main locations. There were two parties, one in South Kensington. (The parties were one of the great reasons for being a member of the Group. Some were listed in the newsletter, but it was more common to put around details by word of mouth). There was an outing to see *A Streetcar Named Desire* at the Piccadilly Theatre, starring Claire Bloom.

The social events consisted of the visit to the GLF Carnival Dance held at the Surrey Halls in Stockwell, an evening trip to the "Old Caledonian" on the Thames near Temple Station (straight pub being zapped, not for the first or last time), a river trip in conjunction with the Bloomsbury Group, and a CHE Lottery Draw at La Chic, Nottingham, which was at that time considered quite a gay place.

This must have been the year of the Malvern CHE Conference, as I remember it being talked about. It was a small do and people seem to have enjoyed themselves and had great fun. (By the time I got to a conference they had become rather dull affairs).

I had my first experience of gay campaigning with SMG (the Scottish Minorities Group—we had to avoid the mention of homosexuality as homosexual acts were still illegal in Scotland). There everything was very relaxed, so it was a great surprise to find that CHE was run much more like a bureaucratic enterprise, somewhere between a government department and the Trades' Union Congress.

Out and About

July/August 1974 featured four talks including ones on human relationships and VD; a summer walk on the Downs; a concert at Kenwood; visits to two plays, *A Worthy Guest* by Paul Bailey, containing a "magnificent naked man" and *Two Noble Kinsmen* at Regents Park—no naked men, but the weather did stay fine; pub visits to the Dove at Hammersmith and the *Old Caledonia* floating pub on the Thames (destroyed by fire a few years later).

There was also a party at 43B Boston Park Road in Brentford. The latter was an almost legendary gay address, where many gay guys stayed over the years—bring a friend, a bottle and 20p.

The excitement in September 1974 was the change to Wednesdays! Speakers included Wallace Grevatt and Rose Robertson on young gays; a Police Chief Inspector on the law regarding homosexuality and its enforcement; and a learned gentleman on the leather scene. On the social side, there was a slide show at a flat at Clapham South (at this time

Clapham and most of south London were considered "the pits" before the yuppies arrived in the eighties—many north Londoners had never been to the south!) followed by drinks in the Windmill on Clapham Common.

In October 1974 there was a talk on "Friend" by Vivian Waldron; a talk by Howarth Penny, General Secretary of CHE; and another personal talk by Jack Dash, the sixties dockers' leader. I remember thinking during this frankly rather embarrassing evening in South Kensington that he could be *heard* in Docklands! Then there were the ever-exciting committee elections, and a theatre visit to *The Mousetrap* (which could have been a member as it was now 21 years old: one of the characters had even been updated to be a lesbian). Finally there was the all-important party.

Let My People Come

In November 1974 the talks were about Gay Switchboard, hairdressing, and the CHE combined subscription system—this may not sound exciting, but it was presented by one of CHE's best looking members who enjoyed making friends with other members. The theatre visit was to the revue/musical *Let My People Come*, which was the most sexually explicit show seen since the end of censorship in the sixties. The CHE Winter Fair and Disco took place on the 23rd at the Conway Hall.

December 1974 featured a Liberal Party speaker, a Catholic priest, and a speaker from NCCL (the National Council for Civil Liberties—now Liberty). There was a "come to the meeting and we will tell you where it is" party, a New Year's Eve party, and a trip to see Alan Ayckbourn's play *Absurd Person Singular*.

January 1975 started with a party, then there were talks on public relations, campaigning, the Metropolitan Community Church, and looking after your teeth. There was an opera evening—*Cavalleria Rusticana* and *Pagliacci* at the Coliseum for the princely sum of £1.00.

February 1975 featured the American gay liberation writer Len Richmond talking on sex, Vivian Waldron on Friend (counselling), and talks on Centre (I cannot remember what this was—presumably some form of counselling/support organisation). There was a party (at the legendary Theatre Street). This was all topped out with two theatre trips, one to *Carmen* at the ENO and one of the great gay legends, Marlene

Dietrich at the Wimbledon Theatre (£2.00 only!). This was her last London appearance, and I am assured that she had to be propped up through the show, but she gave a terrific performance.

Gay Sweatshop

There were some talks—on public relations, the Beaumont Society for transvestites, Nettie Pollard on Icebreakers. There were a couple of parties, another theatre trip to see *John, Paul, George, Ringo and Bert* in Shaftesbury Avenue, and a trip to Woburn followed by dancing the night (well, perhaps only the evening) away in Pan's Club in Luton.

In May 1975 there were talks on the CHE law reform campaign; one given by a beautician; and our old friend, Friend. A basic talk on sex was given with an advanced one promised, which I cannot remember coming to fruition. There was a disco and Theatre Workshop at ULU); a trip to see *Entertaining Mr Sloane* at the Royal Court Theatre; and two parties, one advertised, and one by word of mouth. This was very important for me, as it was there I met the love of my life, Howard.

June 1975 featured a talk by Rose Robertson, one on gay history and a trip to Brixton Gay Community Centre to discuss Gay Liberation. The Cookery Group had a meeting—it was a spin-off from the Young London and other groups. The main event, however, in March 1975 was the founding of the Gay Sweatshop theatre group by Roger Baker. He gave a talk about it and several people attended the first performance—*Thinking Straight* in the Almost Free Theatre in Rupert Street.

Taking Liberties

July 1975 featured another important venture on the gay scene—the first CHE "Liberties" disco at the Hanover Grand. In August the talk was given by Colin Clarke, photographer from *Quorum* magazine—boy, did we preen ourselves in expectation of being selected for his next shoot! September 1975 featured an optician talking about making our eyes look beautiful, a joint meeting with Sappho at the Chepstow starring Quentin Crisp, and a discussion on the future of the Group.

In October 1975 the main event was the decision to change the name from "CHE Youth Group" to "CHE Young London Group". Then there was the question of the definition of "youth". Also there was the desire of some members to remain members of the group beyond the then age limit of 25, which was eventually raised to 30.

Onwards to November 1975 when a group of swimming enthusiasts were trying to get a regular visit to that wonderful Art Deco building, the Marshall Street baths. The Conway Hall hosted the CHE Winter Fair (which we supported), including a disco and a play, *Mr X*, performed by Gay Sweatshop.

There was a Law Reform Mass Rally in Trafalgar Square—I believe this was the occasion we zapped the Charing Cross Station branch of W H Smith, who refused to stock *Gay News*. It shocks me to think that nowadays we have less freedom to demonstrate than thirty years ago.

Campaigning and Camping

In February 1976 there was a demonstration at British Home Stores, Oxford Street, after one of their employees, Tony Whitehead, had been sacked for appearing on a TV programme about gays.

In March there were talks from the Gay Left, on the Grapevine counselling service and a priest discussing the Pope's (Paul VI) statement (the most permanent memory I have of Paul VI was watching his funeral service in a gay sauna in Stockholm). Also advertised in the sheet was the start of "Bang" disco at the Astoria in Tottenham Court Road on Mondays only. Soon Saturdays were added, and so was born one of the legendary gay venues. In its most recent avatar, it was "G-A-Y", a mandatory gig for every major pop star.

April 1976 featured talks on sexual attractiveness, the women's movement, and being a lesbian. In May we had a joint meeting with the Streatham Group in Balham; a talk on the operation of the CHE office (that must have been rivetting!); a debate on forcing gays to come out; and a talk about the CHE NUS Week of Action on Gay Rights (May 10th to 14th). The theatre visit was to see *Equus* featuring Gerry Sundquist—and skating at Queensway ice rink.

The main event in May was the CHE conference in Southampton. My memories are of a guy playing the organ before the main sessions in the

Town Hall. This took place to the backdrop of the Jeremy Thorpe trial, about which no statement was made.

There was a joint women's meeting with the Streatham women's group (I wasn't there, honest!), and a party in Putney. Another legendary event was our theatrical visit to see Barry Humphries at the Globe (now Gielgud) Theatre, with drinks afterwards in the Golden Lion, then renowned as a place to pick up squaddies.

The Sols Arms—a central meeting place

February 1976 saw the first mention of joint ULU Gaysoc/YLG discos to be held on the first Saturday of each month in the Sols Arms (on the corner of Hampstead Road and Drummond Street).

The Sols Arms near Warren Street Underground

It was not a nice pub—straight, modern—but the discos, held in the upstairs room, were quite fun. It was demolished several years ago. It stood near another place popular with gays—Lawrence Corner's military surplus shop, which shut recently. But for the first time we had a definite focal point and in a central venue.

The Sols also had discos on Monday for Gay Alliance, Wednesday for ULU Gaysoc/YLG, Thursday for Sappho, and Fridays for CHE.

Later days of the CHE Young London Group

August 1976 featured talks on Buddhism and the Samaritans, and a visit to the Queen's Head. There was also a protest march starting at Victoria Embankment. This splendid occasion featured an old woman, standing under the statue of Boadicea in her chariot, brandishing an umbrella shouting "you should all be ashamed of yourselves!"

September 1976 saw the usual diet of the Sols Arms disco, plus a couple of interesting talks, one on "young gays" featuring a rent boy, the other on pornography.

It must have been around this time that the decision was made to move meetings to the Crown pub in Edgware Road (now replaced by Marks & Spencer). The format stayed the same—a talk, followed by a few drinks on the premises.

I recall going to a few meetings at the Crown, and indeed I hosted a party for group members when I bought my flat in 1977, but by then I had decided to call it a day. A "young London" group which aged with its members was not a sensible idea.

Today, sadly the Young London Group is no longer in existence, but its early pioneering days were indeed an exciting time. I suppose it was less "stable" in its membership because naturally there was an upper age limit. Also, being full of young males there was inevitably some sexual rivalry, which could lead to tension and friction. But it did give us all the chance to meet off the commercial scene, in a more relaxed and less expensive environment and with a better chance of making real friends.

So on the whole it has left me, and probably many others, with pleasant memories.

Chapter Twenty-Three
The Southwark-Lambeth Group 1976–1980

by Jeff Doorn

In the scorching summer of 1976, Oliver Merrington and Peter Hitcham hosted a meeting of the Southwark/Camberwell section of Lewisham CHE at their Burton Road SW9 flat. This was the forerunner of a new group, to be called Southwark Lambeth Area Gay Society. A newsletter was soon circulated, announcing the inaugural meeting of SLAGS on 1 September at a flat in SE17. We were invited to speak on "What I want SLAGS to be". The consensus was to aim for a balance between social activities and campaigning.

We established a pattern of regular meetings and agreed contacts for National CHE (Peter), Women (Hibby), Streatham CHE (Stuart James) and Lewisham CHE (John Mathewson). Lewisham group donated £20 to help us set up. In October, SLAGS became Southwark/Lambeth CHE, though it was not until the December National Council meeting that we were officially recognised as such. We elected a committee, with Peter as Convenor, Stuart as Membership Secretary and James Farmer as Treasurer. I took on the newsletter from the third (November) issue.

Initially, one fortnightly Wednesday meeting was at our first "permanent" venue, St Giles Centre, Camberwell Church Street, featuring a speaker; the other was a discussion or event at varying venues including Waterloo Action Centre and South Bank Poly Students Union. Speakers ranged from writer and journalist Rictor Norton on "With Breeches Unbuttoned" in 18th century London, to Brian Derbyshire on the leather scene.

From spring 1977 we alternated meetings between Southwark, at the GLC Advice Centre, 29/35 Lordship Lane SE22 (hired free of charge) and Lambeth at Caldwell Street Day Centre, near Clapham Road (75p an evening via the borough's Village Hall Scheme). Subjects at the former included "Revolution or Reform", Icebreakers, married gays, criminal law, censorship and "Childhood Rights". Speakers at the latter included Jackie Forster of Sappho, Tom Jones of the Open Church Group, author Colin

Spencer, Rose Robertson of Parents Enquiry, and Jim Herrick, Secretary of the National Secular Society and editor of *The Freethinker*. Three meetings were held at South Lambeth Tate Library when Caldwell Street was not available. One of these brought Nettie Pollard of NCCL (now Liberty). Looking back, many topics have current or renewed relevance, eg August Trust/Age Concern on housing for elderly gay people and a March 1977 talk on the problems of gay teachers, which was covered by the *South London Press*.

Supporting local discos

Every month we held new members evenings in our homes to welcome people in a relaxed, non-commercial atmosphere. But we also had pub evenings at the Hand in Hand in SE1, the Grove Tavern in Camberwell; the Royal Vauxhall Tavern, the Ship & Whale in SE16, and the Union Tavern in Camberwell New Road.

Union Tavern, Camberwell New Road

Editorial comment on the Union Tavern:

It was exceptional in two ways amongst gay venues. Firstly it was so friendly—always easy to find someone to chat to; there was a very healthy co-existence between the straights and the gays. I remember once walking with a friend into the smaller straight bar by mistake (on the left in the photo), and the landlady said to us "I think you want the other side darlings—it's the butch ones this side!"

Secondly I think it was almost the only London pub where there was disco dancing for the gays downstairs in the main bar, where we would all be bopping about in our green check shirts and flairs, so popular in that era. Half a mile down the road, the Father Redcap on Camberwell Green kept to the usual rule—quiet drinking downstairs and disco dancing upstairs. I think both pubs featured nights by the famous gay dj, Tricky Dicky.

More discos

As a general rule, in the days before the burgeoning club scene, groups ran their own discos. They were fun and friendly, cheap and cheerful, with no attitude, ageism or fashion police. We supported those run by Croydon CHE at the Star, Bexley/Dartford CHE at the Black Prince, Bromley CHE at the Northover pub SE6, and others at the Bull SW14, The Butts at Elephant and Castle, Merton Hall (WAGS) in South Wimbledon, and Lambeth Town Hall (GLF).

We ran our own discos at the Hanover Arms upstairs room at the Oval, "Cuckoo's Nest" at South Bank Poly, and Surrey Halls, Binfield Road Stockwell (including a Christmas disco called "Snow Ball".)

Outings included concerts and theatre trips, e.g. *The Dear Love of Comrades* at Oval House Theatre, and *A Lover and His Lad*, written by a member.

We also joined forces with Croydon CHE to stage Robert Patrick's *The Haunted Host*, which was favourably reviewed in the *Croydon & Purley Advertiser*.

"Mary, Mary, Mary, OUT, OUT, OUT!"

Apart from ongoing issues such as the unequal age of consent (21 for gay men, 16 for everyone else), several campaigns centred around *Gay News*, then the only journal for gay people. In those pre-PC days, anyone who was not "straight" was "gay".

We tried to encourage libraries to stock it and demonstrated against W H Smith for refusing to sell it. In one memorable zap, a group of us brought armfuls of periodicals to the counter of W H Smith's in Beckenham; each was to ask for a copy of *GN*, and when told they did not carry it, would decline to buy the rest. However, some of us quailed, as the clerk was a pretty, young blond! The major attack on *GN* came from Mary Whitehouse's prosecution for blasphemous libel; we joined many protests and benefit evenings. Somewhere in the BBC's vaults is film of us opposite the Old Bailey shouting "Mary, Mary, Mary, OUT, OUT, OUT."

We also lobbied local councillors and MPs, and supported gay rights candidate Peter Mitchell of Westminster CHE in his parliamentary bi-election campaign.

Links and Affiliations

In addition to the CHE links listed above, we affiliated to Southwark Council for Voluntary Services, NCCL and the like. We visited and partied at South London Gay Centre at 78 Railton Road, Brixton, and maintained links with the Brixton Faeries and others in the squats, supported Gay Liberation (South London) at 155 Railton Road and attended discos. Further afield, we looked to twinning arrangements, visiting Hastings CHE and hosting Rotterdam COC.

While members supported anti-fascist rallies, there was some disagreement over whether or not to affiliate to Southwark Campaign Against Racism and Fascism. At first it was decided not to affiliate because of SCARF's emphasis on "smashing" the National Front (predecessor of the BNP); but when SCARF overcame their negative image, we reversed the decision. The controversy generated publicity and public debate, which was all to the good.

Gaining Recognition

We adopted a constitution, held regular committee meetings and elected new committees at AGMs. I became Convenor in autumn 1977; James was elected the following October, when the constitution was suspended as the group became a collective. Stuart James was our final Convenor from autumn 1979. Over the years we took part in Pride marches. As we gathered near Temple station on 25 June 1977, our Convenor was still sewing a shiny orange lambda on our banner! That march, with its rally and picnic in Hyde Park, contrasted with the listless affair from Sloane Square via Chelsea and Earl's Court the next year.

We also participated in CHE National Councils, Winter Fairs and annual conferences in various towns, some more welcoming than others. Our presence anywhere was a statement, from a local fair, where we defied a ban on our banner, to picnics everywhere from Greenwich Park to the concrete area at Waterloo where the Imax now stands. Publicity was important, and we gained recognition and members when *South London Press* accepted our advertisements. Though many people contacted us, and/or attended social events, not everyone joined. Still, we went from an initial seven people to a membership of forty at our peak.

A lasting legacy

Southwark/Lambeth CHE was dissolved on 30 April 1980. Several of our mainstays had moved away, and the remaining active members felt overburdened. Although the group lasted only just under four years, we accomplished a great deal in engaging both gay and straight people, providing encouragement and support in coming out and raising awareness of gay issues.

Relationships blossomed and friendships were formed, many of which continue over thirty years on. Some members went on to join other groups, or had already started other groups,[20] and to continue to press for gay rights.

---

20 See the start of the next chapter, on the Kingston group.

Profiles

Oliver Merrington had come out to his parents in 1973 and joined CHE in 1974. He served on the committee of the CHE Youth Services Information Project and that of ULU Gaysoc. Through a Gaysoc friend he had met Peter, originally from Lowestoft. When they moved to Burton Road, Oliver was a Field Officer for CHE, so it was almost inevitable he would set up a new group in the area. Subsequently, he set up and ran City of London CHE, a joint group with City University Gaysoc. In 1977 Oliver moved to Saffron Walden in Essex and got involved with Cambridge CHE. Later on he helped found the Cambridge AIDS Helpline. He is a member of the Hall-Carpenter Archives, the national lesbian and gay archive, based in London.

I had moved to south London in 1975, though I had previously visited in 1972, dancing in the upstairs disco at the Father Redcap, Camberwell Green. I joined CHE in April 1976 and attended the national conference at Southampton the following month; I came out at work on my return. Joining the new, local group at its first meeting that summer, I went on to produce most issues of the newsletter. I remained an individual CHE member for a few years after the group disbanded.

In 1994 I joined Gay Authors Workshop, which later gave rise to Paradise Press. For a time I was involved with Lambeth LGBT Forum. I became an active member of Southwark LGBT Network and associated with Southwark LGBT Forum (formerly Southwark Anti-Homophobic Forum). In addition, I am a founder member of the Goldies, an over-50s LGBT group supported by Age UK Lambeth. After years of hoarding Southwark-Lambeth newsletters and other material in my loft, I donated the collection to London Metropolitan Archives, where it can be consulted by anyone interested.

Jeff Doorn

Chapter Twenty Four
The Kingston Group 1986–2001

by John Clarke, Gary Mills, and Tony Walton

Beginnings

As early as 1972 there had been a friendly CHE group meeting informally once a month in a flat in Portsmouth Road, Surbiton—part of the London Borough of Kingston and overlooking the Thames. Two members lived in the same block of flats, and so were the nucleus.

Around 1977, about a year after the Surbiton group seems to have faded away, the CHEK group started. This stood for CHE Kingston—and how it came into being has an amusing side to it. A gentleman named Oliver Merrington (mentioned in the last chapter) was keen to get new groups started everywhere: he knew that Peter, who had been a leading light in the Southwark-Lambeth group, had moved to Kingston—so Oliver had Peter's phone number published as someone who could be contacted. The first thing Peter and Victor heard about the Kingston group was people phoning up their home to find out details!

Perhaps because of Peter's background in the Southwark-Lambeth group, there was a commitment to campaigning. In 1978, jointly with CHERP, CHEK organised a petition outside W H Smith's in both Kingston and Richmond in protest at Smith's refusal to stock *Gay News*. The political side of things was always to the fore and they saw themselves as a campaigning group every bit as much as a social group

Very soon the group started to hold their meetings at the Friends Meeting House in Kingston. The venue deserves a place of honour in this book as, along with GALHA at Conway Hall, the Kingston group is the only group in this book to have kept one meeting place for twenty-five years. In fact it was unusual for a group to be able to keep the same meeting place for more than five years.

Speakers at the Friends Meeting House included many political personalities, and also a psychotherapist named Margaret Branch. Another woman speaker was Inspector Cecilia Cundy from the local police, a forceful lady who kept the meeting in very good order! And another was the feminist Wanda Goldwag who had some interestingly left-wing views, as well as the more moderate Jackie Forster.

The Friends (Quakers) Meeting House in Kingston's busy centre

Victor was always very keen to have women in the group but there could occasionally be tension, and this will come up later in the history of KRAGS, which was the successor to CHEK.

Both CHEK and CHERP had banners at Gay Pride, and the only argument was over who should take it home! Eventually the CHEK banner got left on a train (or somewhere) after a march, so there was no banner the following year. The group also got involved in CHE national events – see photos on the next page, of the CHEK stall at the annual fair at Conway Hall, and some members at the national CHE conference in York in 1980.

Congratulations to the Kingston group on being almost the only local group to have kept photos from their seventies/eighties events.

Left: the **CHEK** stall at the annual fair at Conway Hall
Right: members at the National Conference in York, **1980**

Discos and socials

Kingston was and is a very different town from Wimbledon, even though they are close geographically. You will have read in the chapter on WAGS how they had a lot of success setting up local discos in Wimbledon, but with Kingston there was a very conservative council in those days who wanted no night life in the borough at all! A member of the old Surbiton CHE group, who was travelling from Wimbledon in 1972, remembers walking through Surbiton to go to the CHE group meeting at 8 pm and thinking the High Street was like a cemetery.

So it was scarcely surprising that CHEK's attempts at starting a gay disco in the upstairs room of the Griffin pub, by the central market square of Kingston, would run into problems. The Griffin pub itself is now a shop, but the first-floor ballroom which the group used is still intact (see photo).

The landlord there was himself very sympathetic, but he was soon told by the powers-that-be (Chamber of Commerce etc) that if he persisted in allowing gays to use his room they would seek new venues for their business social occasions. It had made headlines in the *Surrey Comet* and had been mentioned on a local radio station, so being too "out" in the suburbs did have its down side, as the Bexley group was also to discover.

The Griffin, close to Kingston's Market Place

After the popular but short-lived disco at the Griffin, a further attempt was made in 1980 to start a CHEK disco at the Grove Tavern in Cambridge Road, Norbiton, but that was near a council estate and again it was maybe doomed to failure because of opposition from locals. The committee decided in the end that Kingston just wasn't the place for such events, and instead they supported the WAGS disco at Merton Hall and later at the Dog & Fox, as well as the GAGS one at the Greyhound, Guildford.

To make up for the setbacks on the disco front, CHEK organised two wonderful riverboat cruises along the Thames from Kingston to Hampton Court and back. There was drinking and dancing on board and eventually even the crew became quite friendly too.

Another very successful social event was when Victor and Peter turned their front room into a restaurant to raise funds for the group, with a ten course meal on offer!

The Beginnings of KRAGS

We have found out quite a bit about the Kingston group in the seventies and quite a bit about the nineties. All we really know about the eighties is that in 1983 the decision was taken to merge CHEK and CHERP and to form the Kingston and Richmond Area Gay Society (KRAGS). This was round about the same time as the collapse of the system of nationwide "CHE groups." No further details have been discovered. The formation of KRAGS was one of the very few examples we know of two London groups merging, and we would love to have known details of how it came about.

We have however located one leaflet describing KRAGS and dating from the early eighties. Here is an extract from it:

"It is because many gays want something more than depending on the gay scene to meet their needs. We all need friends—in some ways our friends can be surrogate families. Belonging to a gay group, such as ours, is a way of meeting new friends and keeping in contact in our local area. Wouldn't it be great to make friends locally who can also share your passions—theatre, film, dance, music, food, gardens, walks etc.?"

A fractious matter in the 1980s, on the other hand, had concerned the women members. Although Philip Bayliss didn't become a member of KRAGS until 1985, he vaguely remembers hearing that, shortly before, there had been a substantial female membership There had been, however, rows over lesbian objections to any hints of female impersonation by men (for instance drag acts, and a regular newsletter gossip column by "Auntie Terry"—no, it wasn't the SLG Terry!).

The female members demanded the right to see an advance copy of the newsletter and censor out things they found offensive. This was refused and the group split, with the lesbians going off to KENRIC.

On a happier note: one of the leading lights at this time was Jack Ellis. He had originally been in CHERP but went on to get involved with KRAGS. He was described by all as a very gentle and pleasant person, who lived in an "olde worlde" cottage in Twickenham, now the Twickenham Museum, by the side of the Thames. John Clarke describes him as "quiet but always warm and sincere." He sadly passed away in 1994.

Later on a member regularly brightened up KRAGS newsletters with his cartoons; we include a few in this chapter, as they were an almost unique feature. The talented cartoonist, now an SLG member, has given us permission to include them but would prefer to remain anonymous.

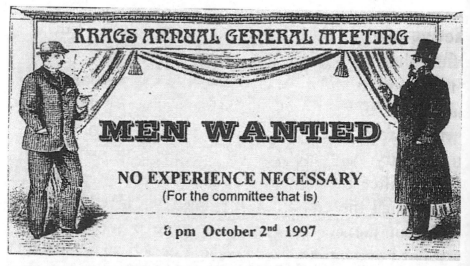

John Clarke and the nineties

Gary Mills gives us some more memories of KRAGS in the 1990s

Happiest memories were the monthly speaker meetings that John Clarke, then convenor, arranged from 1994 at the Friends Meeting House in Eden Street, Kingston. He got remarkably good speakers. Duncan Lustig-Prean (of the Stonewall four) attracted press reporters and a press photographer. He spoke very well on the issue of gays being banned from the military.

Rev Richard Kirker attracted the press and an attendance of thirty, when homosexuality and the Church were hot topics.

Our second cartoon shows convenor John Clarke being firm with some politicians.

KRAGS 23rd YEAR   SEPTEMBER 1995

PROBE THE POLITICIANS ON GAY ISSUES
AT THE MONTHLY MEETING.

But the meeting I remember best was with Alan Bray who spoke on same sex partnerships in history. Alan knew he would die before the publication of his book, but he was fascinating—and *The Friend* (Chicago Press c2002) was one of the best reads I've ever had.

John Clarke was a member of the Oscar Wilde Society, and wrote the script for a play reading on Wilde for the anniversary of the famous trials and imprisonment in 1895. I took part (and provided the green carnations). It was performed by two professional actors at the Friends Meeting House.

John also organised two Oscar Wilde walks around London. Our cartoonist gave a version of the famous portrait.

KRAGS 23rd YEAR   MAY 1995

Other highlights

When John Clarke took over as convenor in 1994 he took the decision to have speakers again at the monthly meetings, because over the previous few years they had been having mainly general discussions or cheese and wine parties. But social events continued much as before. For example classical music evenings over in Tolworth at Graham's home were very successful, and these were to continue after the group had closed down.

Pub evenings were a regular part of the KRAGS programme, including visits to the Bridge bar in Fulham and the Reflex in Putney. Sadly the dear old Imperial in Richmond had closed down in about 1992, but the Richmond Arms became a regular venue in its stead. Occasionally we would join the Guildford group for a pub evening at the Greyhound.

One very successful meeting was the visit by LAGPA (L & G Police Association). The speaker told us how a group within the police had stood up to a homophobic chief constable and forced him to change his attitude.

So although KRAGS always maintained it was not a campaigning group, it took an interest in matters of concern. The evening's subject prompted another successful cartoon.

KRAGS 23rd YEAR   MARCH 1995

Another interesting feature of the newsletter was something called "Grapevine". This was an opportunity for members to chat about any matters of interest. There was also a very balanced programme in the newsletter with events titled "Social KRAGS", "Bopping KRAGS", "Political KRAGS" and so on. A regular monthly event was the visit to Ralph's cellar bar disco in Farnham, with members arranging lifts in cars.

On most New Year's Days there was for a time a group walk out into Surrey. There were regular barbecues at Ron's during the summer and, on several Mayday Bank Holidays, KRAGS had a stall at the Kingston Green Fair in Canbury Gardens.

The 25th anniversary was held in 1997, since the Richmond bit of the group had, as we have seen in the earlier chapter on Wandsworth-Richmond, started back in 1972. The anniversary was a big occasion with a garden party in the Unitarian Church garden in Ormond Road, Richmond, and later a dinner in the Dysart Arms, Petersham.

In October 1997 there was a visit to Wimbledon Theatre to see Hinge and Bracket, a part of their "champagne tour" which may well have been their last.[21]

The Group's final big "do" was on 31 July 1999, when KRAGS were back at the Unitarian Church garden in Richmond. Stephen Twigg, MP, opened the event.

Back to Gary:

Meetings continued on the first Thursday in the month at the Friends Meeting House. But the attendance at the meetings was at this time very worrying, and we were often embarrassed that John would invite excellent speakers and we could hardly justify their attendance.

The decision to close the group down was finally taken in 2001. The group's funds were distributed between various gay charities, and some of the remaining members joined South London Gays.

But many warm and happy memories remain of the KRAGS group and of CHEK before it, both centred (amazingly for 25 years) on meetings at the Friends Meeting House in Eden Street, Kingston.

---

[21] In Chapter One you may have read that Hinge & Bracket, then an almost unknown duo, went to the SK group to entertain them in about 1971. There's quite a big gap between those two dates!

Chapter Twenty-Five
3F (LGCM London) 1977–

This includes a short section on the London
Lesbian & Gay Centre in Cowcross Street[22]

LGCM (the Lesbian and Gay Christian Movement) had been founded in 1976, with its inaugural general meeting at a primary school very near to St Botolph's, Aldgate. There was soon a move to set up groups on a local basis, in the same way as CHE had done shortly before that time. 3F, the nearest LGCM group to Central London, was amongst the first to be formed, and it was originally called the Central London group.

3F was started partly by Malcolm Johnson who had also been one of the key players with the SK group but, as he was still strongly involved in the SK group and other projects, he understandably said that he didn't want to be the convenor. Richard Kirker was probably the first convenor, although on his own admission he cannot quite remember!

The group started in 1977 in St Botolph's Aldgate crypt, with Malcolm Johnson, the Rector, acting as host. The name 3F was adopted as it met on the third Friday in the month—this is another connection with SK because the emphasis seems to have been to provide something for the weekend, 3F being on Friday and SK on a Saturday! The other connections between the two groups are that they both started in the Aldgate/Limehouse part of London, and they both in their early days involved Malcolm Johnson.

So 3F had been formed as the LGCM group for Central London, especially for those working in London. For the latter reason it used to have the early starting time of 7.30 p.m., and many members used to be dressed in business suits—they were in the majority right up until the 1990s!

---

[22] Although this is chronologically Chapter 25, it was in fact the first or second chapter to be written: it appeared for 3F's thirtieth birthday, and the booklet where it was published inspired the idea of this book.

In 1980 3F moved to Queen Mary College, East London, where Malcolm had been the chaplain. Then, in 1983, we changed to St James's Piccadilly, a much more centrally situated venue, where we met in the Wren Café.

St James's Church Piccadilly, showing the Wren Café

Several other LGCM groups started in London at about the same time as 3F (or maybe a little bit later), a particularly successful one being the South West London group, which met under the auspices of Rev John Cuthbert at the Church of the Ascension on Lavender Hill, or occasionally in Stoneleigh, Surrey, at the home of the convenor. There were also groups in West, North and East London, but by 2000 the only one left in Greater London was 3F.

In those early days, when Richard Kirker had (probably!) been the convenor, the emphasis had been on finding top rate speakers on subjects of interest—they had included Alan Webster (Dean of St Paul's) as well as Edward Carpenter (Dean of Westminster and descendant of the original

Edward Carpenter). We also had Richard Dyer, talking to us about films of interest to gays and showing us extracts.

The Cecil Rowe Years

Cecil Rowe now takes up the story for himself:

I had just come out of the closet, was getting divorced, and in 1984 I went to see Richard Kirker to find out what the Gay Christian movement was all about.

Richard told me about the 3F group, at that time meeting at the coffee shop attached to St James's Piccadilly, and I duly went along, only to find, from the convenor running the group that evening, that unless someone else took over as convenor that would be the last 3F meeting! I faintly recall that the subject of the evening had been homoeroticism in Western art and I thoroughly enjoyed myself. This was after all my first chance to actually meet other gay Christians.

I am not sure what possessed me but I decided there and then to take up the reins and keep 3F ticking over in the absence of anyone else offering to do so. As I recall, after a couple more meetings at St James's Church, we re-launched 3F at the London Lesbian and Gay Centre in Cowcross Street in March 1985. The title of our first meeting there was "Coming Out—is it worth it?"

The London Lesbian and Gay Centre 1983–1992

Editor's diversion: A short break to talk about the Gay Centre, where 3F, along with many other groups, used to meet.

The subject of the LLG Centre could fill another book, but we'd like to record what happy memories many gays have of it during its short life, and how sad it is that London should now be one of the few European capitals without such a Centre.

It was closed down partly perhaps through the rather amateurish, left-wing way it was organised, but also mainly because the Tory government was having a vendetta against Ken Livingstone and his use of ratepayers' money in London for such projects. When the GLC was abolished by Mrs Thatcher, and powers handed over to the London boroughs, almost all buildings let out by the GLC were transferred to the boroughs except for—can't you guess? —yes, the LLG Centre. The excuse was that it had to be commercially viable. Fair enough, and therefore the obvious thing was for them to ask for the Centre to be run on a viable instead of a subsidised basis. Instead of that it was shut down, with almost no notice.

The London Lesbian & Gay Centre, Cowcross Street
(The Centre was the first building on the left in this photo, with Farringdon Station the white building on the right)

It was sad also for 3F, as a lot of visitors would get to hear about it there and come along to the meetings—I myself, like many others, heard about 3F through seeing a notice in the Centre advertising its meetings.

Still on the subject of the LLG Centre, Cecil recommences:

One of the lovely things about the LLG Centre was that before and after 3F meetings there were all the facilities around, which we could enjoy without having to leave the building. This really did help to knit the group together because one could meet for coffee in the café before the start of the meeting, or stay for a meal, a drink or even a disco after the meeting was over.

We stayed on at the Centre for an incredible seven years. Highlights from that period included a series of talks from the religious correspondents of *The Times*, *Telegraph* and *Independent*. Emmanuel Cooper, the arts correspondent of *Gay Times*, gave a talk entitled "Fully Exposed—the male nude in photography." Terence Davies, film maker and director of *Distant Voices, Still Lives* talked about losing his faith, and Peter Tatchell talked about "Europe—the Battle Ground for Equality."

One evening I shall never forget was a very well attended presentation by a gay strip-tease dancer telling us how he was able to reconcile his work with his faith. His presentation culminated in a simulated ejaculation that spattered the front row of the assembled (some of them first-timers) and by now speechless 3F members! I must say numbers then picked up remarkably.

The third Friday in the month at the LLG Centre happened to coincide with the Gummi Group's monthly event—rubber or PVC was their big thing. It was not uncommon to see the odd gay Christian in open sandals and a woolly jumper deep in conversation with a tattooed, pierced man in a shiny black vest.

Like everyone else we were very saddened when the Centre was forced to close down in late 1991 or early 1992.

Various Venues

So 3F had to move on again. We went briefly to the Chalk Farm pub at Regents Park Road, Primrose Hill. It was a pleasant venue, convenient for me as I lived round the corner, but not a venue we could sustain, since it was too far from central London for most 3F punters, who came from all over the capital.

One of the most memorable meetings during that period was a meal organised by the convenor of the Jewish Gay Group: he took us through the Passover meal, describing in great detail the symbolism of the lamb, the unleavened bread, the bitter herbs and so on—such a lovely combination of spiritual and physical sustenance.

Around September 1993 3F moved to the Room Upstairs at Central Station (a gay pub in Wharfdale Road, Kings Cross, formerly the Prince Albert) where we continued to meet until November 1995.

Highlights from that period included Rev Jeffrey John talking about monogamy as the Christian model for gay relationships, in a talk entitled "Permanent, Faithful, Stable," and Mary Loudon talking about her book with the rather intriguing title of "Revelations—the Clergy Questioned." One hopes they weren't too blunt in the questions they asked the clergy!

Then three 3F members—Adam Clark, Tony Dines and Brian Smith—collaborated on an evening called "Towards a Sexual Ethic for Lesbians and Gays."

Incidentally, attempts were made during two periods in the nineties to start a "OneF" evening, with the aim of 3F members purely socialising on the first Friday in the month—first attempts were in about 1992 at the Chalk Farm pub and the second in about 1996 at the Clock House pub, Clapham. Both attempts were abandoned as almost no one was turning up—3F members do seem to like listening to speakers more than anything else, although there was the added difficulty of the two pub venues not being central enough for many of the members. It might have worked better at the Central Station pub, Kings Cross—who knows?

In December 1995 3F moved again, this time to a beautiful room, if somewhat noisy when the windows were left open, at St Anne's Church, Soho. Mind you, being in Soho did have certain social advantages for our members! During 3F's sojourn at St Anne's highlights included a talk by a sex worker, amongst whose clients was an Anglican priest. Then Christopher O'Hare, a TV producer, talked on his programme *Better Dead Than Gay* about Simon Harvey, who so feared his sexuality that he took his own life, aged 26.

That year, 1996, drew to a magnificent close with the Service of Thanksgiving at Southwark Cathedral to celebrate LGCM's twentieth anniversary year. And it must have been sometime during 1996 that I decided, after almost thirteen years at the helm, to bow out.

Many thanks to Cecil for this account.

In about 1997 3F moved (still always on the third Friday) to the Grosvenor Chapel in Mayfair, with Drew Payne as convenor and Howard Cooper as chairman. It was a very pleasant venue, although a longish walk from the nearest tube at Green Park.

Some of the events held at that venue were a talk by Peter Tatchell, recommending there should be a standard age of consent of fourteen for both heterosexuals and homosexuals, another by Geoffrey Duncan entitled "Courage to Love," which was the name of his anthology, and another by the Rev Jean Mayland on "Growing into the image and likeness of God."

Around the end of our time at the Grosvenor Chapel, John Bamford became convenor, Tony Somerton chairman, and Richard Weston treasurer.

Back to St Botolph's!

In 2002 we took the decision to go back to St Botolph's, Aldgate. Some members attended St Botts on a Sunday which made it a natural link, there was an underground station right next door, and it was also a great help having the organist of St Botolph's as our convenor! (By this time, by the way, 3F was being run by a committee and there was general agreement that we never wanted to go back to the old system of the convenor doing everything—excellent though all our convenors had been).

This time round we were in the main body of St Botolph's rather than the crypt. We remember having to share the St Botolph's evenings with the bell-ringers who always practised on Fridays—that could sometimes be a bit difficult although everyone got on well. (You would stand at the door and ask all-comers "Are you a bell ringer or a three-effer?"—it was funny how often you guessed wrongly!).

Our earliest speaker-highlights back at St Botolph's were: Cecil Rowe talking about growing up gay in South Africa; Alastair Duncan talking about The Food Chain for HIV/AIDS sufferers; and Sue Sanders telling us about her organisation to combat homophobia in the classroom, called

Schools OUT. We were also very pleased to welcome Adnan Ali from the Gay Muslim Group, and Dennis Candy telling us about Buddhism.

St Botolph's Church Aldgate

Shortly after the move back to St Botolph's we celebrated our 25th anniversary in 2002, with Malcolm Johnson as our guest speaker. People will remember all the trouble he had been through when Rector of St Botolph's when he had allowed LGCM to have an office there. He had incurred the wrath of the Archdeacon of London, whom some people felt was using technicalities as a pretext for getting LGCM out.

It had been the first time that we'd realised that some conservative evangelicals within the church were starting an organised campaign against gay Christians, and it was a very stressful time for Malcolm Johnson in particular. So we were delighted to welcome him back on this 25th Anniversary—both to 3F and to St Botolph's.

Two years after the 25th Anniversary, and following a very great deal of discussion, it was decided to change the 3F meeting night to the third Thursday instead of the third Friday. The main argument for the change was that it was felt people didn't want to attend meetings at the start of the weekend when they would be doing other things—and it was a very strong argument.

We were all, however, reluctant to change the name of 3F and were grateful to a member, Kristian, who came up with the idea of making the 3F stand for "Third Fellowship," since we would be continuing to meet on the third "whatever" of the month, even though it was no longer a Friday.

Later speakers of special interest were: Jeremy Marks talking on Courage UK, an organisation which originally tried to "cure" evangelical Christians of gayness but finished up completely changing its own views (see Chapter 28), James Baaden of the South London Synagogue telling us about his beliefs, Adam Clark talking about his fascinating work as a life coach, and Steve Brown giving us a well-researched talk on "The Life and Times of Joe Orton."

3F has always been noted for the openness of its discussions and for its interesting speakers on a wide variety of subjects. It has not always been possible to have a speaker on the "gay Christian" aspect, but we have usually managed to find subjects of interest to gay Christians, who are noted for not being narrow-minded. We were once told by someone that we were not sufficiently "spiritually minded"—this was after he had attended a 3F talk on pantomime dames by Royston Kean, entitled "Widow Twanky Reveals All." The talk was extremely good, and we decided to ignore the criticism!

To keep things in balance, however, we were grateful to Rev Keith John who led us in some evenings of spirituality, which we much appreciated.

One decision we took was to join SLAGO—Surrey & London Association of Gay Organisations.—SLAGO is a loose-knit federation of several gay organisations in London, including the Metropolitan Community Church. The idea was to give us the kind of contact with other organisations which 3F had enjoyed so much when at the LLG Centre in Cowcross Street.

A very successful thing we did annually was to have a picnic in August on Hampstead Heath when we used to sit by the lake and listen to the concerts at Kenwood. It was sad that these events were cancelled for a few years but we were glad to hear of their return.

Over the two years from 2005, 3F has welcomed: Peter Robins, the well-known gay author; Ray Gosling of Gay Monitor on his work amongst gays falling foul of the law; Rev Jide Macaulay talking about issues around gay black people, Captain Robin Bates of the Church Army telling us about its work with homeless people; as well as Rev Rose Wilkin of Hackney talking about gang culture and the wonderfully brave work she was doing to tackle it.

Any readers interested in coming along to 3F can find details on the LGCM website, e-mail us on **central.london@lgcm.org.uk**, or contact the LGCM office. At the time of going to press we are still meeting on the third Thursday of every month at St Botolph's Aldgate. But however you find us, you will be made very welcome.

We were very grateful to the following for giving us their recollections of the group's history: Malcolm Johnson, Richard Kirker, Robert Liston, Cecil Rowe, Jeremy T and Richard Weston.

Chapter Twenty-Six

Gay & Lesbian Humanist Association 1979–

by George Broadhead

GALHA is a national organisation but holds its main meeting in London. This account concentrates on its activities in the capital. George Broadhead, a founder member, former long-serving secretary and now a vice-president, looks back at the first ten years of its existence.

George Broadhead

With the exception of the Campaign for Homosexual Equality, the Gay and Lesbian Humanist Association (GALHA) is the longest-established national, secular organisation for lesbians and gays in the UK.

For many years it has held meetings at the Conway Hall, Red Lion Square, the London headquarters of the National Secular Society, and shares the honour, with Kingston, of having kept its meeting place the longest of all the gay groups.

The Beginnings

In the aftermath of the notorious *Gay News* blasphemy trial in 1977, a few gay Humanists, including myself and partner Roy Saich, who were involved in gay rights campaigning, discussed informally the possibility of setting up a gay Humanist group, there being already groups for religious gays.

During the trial, Mrs Mary Whitehouse, who brought the private prosecution against *Gay News*, complained publicly about the opposition to her action from the "gay humanist lobby". There was no such lobby at the time, but her complaint provided the necessary spark. We felt that the aims of such a lobbying group might be threefold:

1) to make gays more aware of the Humanist ethical outlook, which has an enlightened liberal stance on sexual morality;

2) to make heterosexual Humanists more aware of the prejudice and discrimination suffered by gays;

3) To encourage practical Humanist support for the campaign for gay rights.

Vanguard of Protest

In the summer of 1978, at the CHE conference in Coventry, a Humanist stall was set up and a fringe meeting held. The aims were to explore further the need for an organised group. In the same year, Terry Sanderson, now well known as a gay journalist and author, had a thought-provoking article published in *Gay News* on the personal advantages and feeling of liberation provided by the Humanist outlook.

In May 1979 an ad hoc committee decided to use the name Gay Humanist Group (GHG). It was resolved to get a leaflet printed and circulated among interested individuals as well as many gay and humanist groups and publications. Several thousand of these leaflets were distributed at the London Gay Pride march in June (a march which was exceptionally well supported for that time, with some eight thousand people).

In August the group was formally launched at a fringe meeting held at the CHE conference in Brighton. Though fewer than in previous years, there were still about 600 delegates at this conference, and the Humanist meeting was addressed by the editor of *The Freethinker*, Bill McIlroy. We were in the vanguard of protest which greeted the anti-gay statement filling half a page of a Brighton newspaper and signed by 22 of the town's church leaders.

A Time of Growth

As the membership began to grow and as many lived in the Greater London area, it was decided in 1979 to start holding regular monthly public meetings at Conway Hall Humanist Centre, Holborn. This is owned by South Place Ethical Society and as a kindred Humanist organisation, we were able to hire its spacious library for meetings at a very favourable rate.

The Conway Hall, Red Lion Square, Holborn

The first meeting at the Conway Hall featured a talk by the group's president, the lesbian author Maureen Duffy. Her talk "Separate Development: Out of the Closet into the Ghetto" was attended by around 70 people, and resulted in her being interviewed on London Weekend Television.

Other notable speakers at these meetings during the group's first ten years included Antony Grey of the Homosexual Law Reform Society and the Albany Trust; Vitto Russo, the American author of *The Celluloid Closet*; Maureen Colquhoun, the out lesbian Labour MP; Derek Jarman, the gay film director; Francis King, the gay novelist; Andrew Hodges, the gay biographer of Alan Turing; Emmanuel Cooper, the gay art expert; Fiona Cooper, the lesbian author; Stephen Coote, editor of *The Penguin Book of Homosexual Verse*.

The group also arranged a series of talks at Conway Hall entitled "Famous Gay Humanists" and (later) "Lesbians and Gays in the Humanist Tradition". Subjects of these talks included the writers John Addington Symonds, E M Forster, Gore Vidal, Sir Angus Wilson, Marguerite Yourcenar, and John Maynard Keynes.

Other very popular meetings were forums (sometimes just ahead of general elections) with a panel of speakers.

Members of the first elected committee included Trevor Thomas, already a charismatic figure in CHE, Julian Meldrum, later to launch the gay archive project and make a reputation for himself in the field of AIDS, and Jim Herrick, well-known in the Humanist movement and later to become editor of *New Humanist* magazine.

Protest

In 1980 we made a submission to the Home Office committee of enquiry concerning the age of consent and another to CHE about the direction the gay movement should take in the coming decade. We also started publishing a newsletter and got requests to provide speakers for other gay and Humanist groups. We took part in the Gay Pride march with a newly-made banner, and set up a stall at the ULU) building afterwards.

The GALHA banner in Hyde Park, before the 1988 Pride March

In 1981 we sent a submission to the Government's Criminal Law Revision Committee on Sexual Offences. Our Gay Pride meeting that year was addressed by out lesbian and former Labour MP Maureen Colquhoun who said that Britain's gay population "must begin showing signs of political muscle if it is to survive in a society which looks like becoming more and more hostile".

In 1982 in anticipation of Pope John Paul II's visit to Britain, we launched POPE: People Protesting at Papal Edicts, and provoked an outburst from arch-homophobe Sir John Junor, editor of the *Sunday Express*.

Our President, Maureen Duffy, addressed our Pride meeting the same year and called on GHG and the gay rights movement as a whole to campaign for the removal of the discriminatory age of consent affecting gay men.

In 1983, following the proposed outreach by the Metropolitan Community Church in London gay bars, we challenged the MCC to a debate. By this time our newsletter had become a magazine with news, features and reviews, including a regular TV/film column by Jonathan Sanders, later to become TV critic for *Gay Times*.

In 1984 we published a booklet *Secular Humanism* by Kit Mouat, and sent a letter of complaint to Cardinal Basil Hume following a statement from the Vatican describing homosexuality as "a moral disorder". We acquired a panel of vice-presidents including jazz singer George Melly. We held a joint meeting with the Gay Black Group at the Conway Hall. We arranged the first of our annual residential weekend gatherings.

In 1985 we made a submission to the working party drafting the GLC's charter for Gay and Lesbian Rights, and thwarted attempts by gay Christians (notably the Metropolitan Community Church) to water down the section on "Organised Religion".

There was always a social side to our group and that year we held our first Winter Solstice party in January. We also celebrated our fifth anniversary with a party at Conway Hall.

The Late Eighties and Clause 28

1986 was a very busy year of campaigning for GHG in many geographical areas. We made a strong protest to a West Midlands councillor who claimed that God has sent AIDS to get rid of "poofs and queers", and managed to get a homophobic recorded phone message advertised by Birmingham Christadelphians withdrawn. We also got a bus-load of GHG members to descend on Nottingham with a banner to take part in a rally protesting at the Labour Council's veto on lesbian and gay equal opportunities.

In 1987 a Vatican document described "the particular inclination of the homosexual" as "a more or less strong tendency towards an intrinsically moral evil". In a press release GHG commented in reply: "The sophistry which allows the Roman Catholic Church to condemn homosexuality as evil, while calling on its priests to provide pastoral care, is utterly contemptible."

This was a decade over-shadowed by AIDS, and our president Maureen Duffy was one of the speakers at the Terrence Higgins Trust candlelight gathering in London's Jubilee Gardens in 1987. And still on the subject of AIDS we strongly condemned the anti-gay "cesspit" speech of James Anderton, Chief Constable of Greater Manchester.

We devised a Humanist "affirmation" ceremony of love and commitment for lesbian and gay couples as an alternative to the Christian "blessing" performed by some clergy. Part of our ceremony was used by Channel 4's Network 7 programme, which featured the first close-up gay smoocher on TV and provoked outrage from Mary Whitehouse and her supporters in Parliament.

We held a Special General Meeting at Conway Hall in 1987 to change our name from Gay Humanist Group (GHG) to Gay and Lesbian Humanist Association (GALHA).

In 1988 several Humanist organisations publicly declared their opposition to the anti-gay Clause 28 in the Conservative Government's Local Government Act, and GALHA took part with its banner in the large demonstration held against this clause in Manchester. Maureen Duffy successfully proposed a motion at the TUC in the same year deploring the passing of Section 28 as an infringement of the basic right to free speech and expression.

For the third successive year, in 1988 we co-sponsored with CHE the London Lesbian and Gay Winter Fayre, which was held at the GLC's County Hall.

In 1989 we issued a statement defending author Salman Rushdie against death threats from Islamic fundamentalists, and another supporting the Campaign Against Blasphemy Law in its opposition to extension of this law. We also protested about the activities of a Christian "counselling" service called U-Turn Anglia which sought to change gays from their "wicked ways". Also in 1989 we held a very well attended reception at Conway Hall to mark our tenth anniversary.

Anyone wanting information about GALHA or wanting to join can contact us by e-mail at **info@galha.org** or view the website, **www.galha.org**.

Chapter Twenty-Seven
SAGO / SLAGO 1984–

Decline and (almost) fall of CHE

In August 1980 the decision was taken at the York CHE conference to radically change CHE. The basic principle of the change was that the two sides of CHE—the campaigning side and the local groups side—would be best separated. The campaigning side would continue as CHE, but the local groups side would be represented by GCO (Gay Community Organisation). With hindsight, one has to say that the decision was probably a disaster and, in almost everyone's opinion now, it would have been better to leave things as they were. But what was done, was done.

The quarterly National CHE Council in March 1982 approved in principle the transfer of local groups to GCO. The break-up was finalised in September 1982 when the arrangement for remitting part of the CHE subscription was done away with. GCO, however, sadly hardly even managed to get itself launched, and a wag (in both senses) named Simon referred to it as a "punctured rubber dinghy attempting to be an ocean liner." Sadly he was just about right, and GCO sank without trace in September 1984.

The campaigning side also suffered, as there was no longer the same support for it from the groups at local level, no longer the huge membership lists to consult if organising a fund-raising fair or conference, and no longer any easy way of sharing expertise. Above all, the taking away of campaigning from the locals groups left them, at least initially, almost without the common cause, common allegiance and comradeship which campaigning had brought.

Picking up the pieces

So there we were, in 1981, with many of the former CHE groups isolated from each other but not really wanting to be.

It would be misleading to suggest that liaison organisations such as SAGO came into being because of the breakup of CHE, since moves towards degrees of federalism had started already, but nevertheless it was fortuitous that in the South London/Surrey area we were not left as isolated from each other as former CHE groups were in other part of the capital, or indeed the rest of the country, after the break-up.

In our area/region discussions had been going on for some time—perhaps because we had been aware for a while that things were radically changing. Luckily enough, there had always been friendly contact between the groups, going back to 1974, and including groups such as Magnet (Bexley & Bromley), Croydon, Streatham and Wimbledon. Both the Croydon disco at the Star and the WAGS disco at Merton Hall had become popular venues for most of the groups in the area. In addition, between 1975 and 1979 a series of South London fund-raising discos were started at the Surrey Halls, Stockwell, which were organised jointly by Croydon, Lewisham and Streatham, only coming to an end as the Halls became too expensive.

In March 1980 a Southern Counties Spring Fayre was held in Croydon Parish Church. Inter-group co-operation continued with a Surrey Regional meeting in Guildford in June 1980, with eleven groups invited from as far afield as Brighton. Proposals were made for joint advertising and a social broadsheet. In December of that year Surrey Gay Link was officially launched. A Surrey Gay Youth Group was to be started, to be overseen by Surrey Gay Link.

During 1981 Surrey Gay Link was effectively replaced by SAGO. The latter was really the committees of the already existing groups starting to keep in touch with each other through a loose knit federation, rather than having something imposed upon them. It stood for "Surrey Area Gay Organisations", although Ray Amer of Croydon felt SAGO was a good name in itself—like little bits of pudding clinging onto each other, he said!

The first members of SAGO were Croydon CHE, GAGS, KRAGS, South Bank Poly Gaysoc and WAGS. The first SLAGO organiser was Timothy Jones, with strong back-up from Mike Harvey and Ray Amer of the Croydon group. Liaison meetings were held at MCC, as Balham was a conveniently central venue and often available (in those days MCC had their own premises in Sistova Road). Timothy Spiers was the rep for MCC, with Peter Kinloch representing Croydon, Mike Goldsmith and Terry

Murphy representing Wimbledon and later Roy Nixon representing CAGY. Very soon the name was changed to Surrey and South West London Area Gay Organisations to give it more accuracy, although the acronym remained SAGO for some years longer. Tony took over as organiser in 1987.

The Croydon group was also involved with SEGG, which stood for South Eastern Gay Groups., and SEGG issued stickers to be stuck onto the back of the various membership cards issued by the different groups to allow entry to events run by other SEGG groups—Tunbridge Wells, Hastings, East Kent, Magic (Medway), Badgers (Bexley and Dartford) and Maidstone Gay Switchboard.

The SAGO Cup

In 1984 WAGS donated the SAGO cup, and Croydon Friend later donated the runner-up trophy. So the annual SAGO cup competition was born, with events (which sound very ambitious now) such as squash and badminton held at Tolworth Recreation Centre, a SAGO sports day (with three legged races and so on), held one sunny summer afternoon in 1987 on Wimbledon Common, and even a swimming gala at Tooting Bec Lido! (As you might have guessed, the average age in groups during the eighties was about fifteen to twenty years younger than in 2010).

For most of the nineties, however, we settled down to a pattern of annual matches, which were hosted as follows: badminton tournament by CAGS at St John's Church, Sylvan Road (Upper Norwood), table tennis tournament by WAGS at the Wimbledon Labour Hall, quiz by LMG at the Locomotive in Camden Town, and ten-pin bowling by KRAGS at Tolworth Bowling Alley.

At the time of going to print, LMG was the holder of the SLAGO cup and 3F the holder of the runners-up trophy. We had not had any sporting events for several years, although in 2010 a successful SLAGO groups table tennis tournament was held in Mitcham. It was hoped this could be the start of other annual events in addition to the very successful quizzes.

In about 1998 GAGS had decided to drop out as they felt they were too far away from the other groups, but on the other hand the London

Monday Group had joined in 1990, and they were to produce our longest serving and invaluable organiser, Brian Parker.

Social Intercourse

Until 2000, Philip Bayliss very efficiently produced SLAGO Link, a newsletter sent to the committees of all the groups to keep them informed of what was going on, both with SAGO's and with other groups' events. He was succeeded in 2000 by Ross Burgess who has held the post equally efficiently ever since, although it has now been replaced by the "SLAGO programme" page on the website.

Now what about discos? That seemingly so easy way to get gays together in the seventies was in a state of fast decline by the mid-eighties. If SAGO had started in 1975 there would have been a hugely successful monthly joint disco being run in Thornton Heath, or Balham or at the White Lion, Putney, with people streaming in from all the local groups. But local gay discos (someone else must find the reasons) faded away, really quite suddenly and finally, around 1985.

The Two Brewers, Clapham High Street

So another form of socialising was needed. This was the monthly SAGO pub evening on the second Friday at the Two Brewers, Clapham.

The informal meetings at the Two Brewers were held in the back bar where, because it was less than half-full till the drag acts started at 11 pm, we could easily find a spare table or two for us all to gather round if we arrived before nine. Those who wanted to stay on for the drag show could do so, and it was a pleasant and well-attended monthly night out. Another very popular and convivial venue for occasional joint pub evenings was the Penny Farthing in Hammersmith, an excellent gay pub which unfortunately disappeared around the turn of this century.

St John's Upper Norwood, mentioned above, became a favourite venue for a number of events, not just for the badminton tournaments but also for a music evening organised by Croydon Friend and (unbelievably) for a revue put on by Harrow Gay Unity in 1990! (We would like to pay tribute to the vicar there, Rev David Martin who, although straight himself, was hugely supportive of gay people. He sadly passed away around 1995 and was much missed).

In 1991, Brian Parker had taken over as SAGO organiser, a post which he has held ever since, with Tony becoming Treasurer. Later Peter Robins became president for a number of years.

Shortly afterwards in 1992 the decision was taken to change the name to Surrey and London Association of Gay Organisations, or SLAGO. This was a sensible move, since several of the member groups were based in London and a long way from Surrey. The only problem with the new name, however, is that it has become permanently confused with SLG (South London Gays) as soon as SLG started three years later. So just to put the record straight, SLG is a member of SLAGO but they are two different things!

There were always one-off events organised by individual groups for the benefit of all the SLAGO groups, such as a treasure hunt organised by the Magnet group at Greenwich, a concert by the American Blues singer Dolores Berry at MCC Balham, a talk by Des on the theatre at Wimbledon, charades by CAGY at the ACE Centre in Croydon, and a Christmas party held by Libertines at Catford.

One stalwart effort was a SLAGO fair, held in March 1996 at the Church of the Ascension, Lavender Hill, and organised by Tony. It was well attended by local bargain hunters and made a profit, but it wasn't supported by many gays, other than the faithful committee members of the individual groups, so we gave up on that idea.

It looks as though by the end of the last century "gay fairs" were coming to an end, rather as "gay discos" had done. One should mention the Rainbow Fairs held at the Waterloo Action Centre in the first three years of the new century, organised by Peter Robins and Alan Louis, which were successful and pleasant events but attracted much fewer numbers than we used to get at Conway Hall and ULU in the seventies and eighties.

The Late Nineties

By the mid-nineties the three most regular events—the monthly get-together at the Two Brewers, badminton at St John's, Upper Norwood and the final quiz at MCC had all come to an end—the Brewers was completely re-shaped and MCC had left their premises at Sistova Road. (By the way, MCC are thanked warmly for all the hospitality, both for liaison meetings and for quizzes, that they gave to SAGO/SLAGO over the years).

Wednesday SLAGO pub evenings were then held at the agreeable Goose & Carrot in Croydon—perhaps assisted by the opening of the tram link—and some successful early inter-group quiz evenings were held in the cellar bar there, organised very capably by Reg Jones. (Sadly the Goose & Carrot was swept away for re-development).

Equally successful, the annual SLAGO day trip to Brighton started in May 1997. (Apparently several GAGS members came on the first one, even though their group was soon to leave SLAGO). On the first one, ribbons had to be worn (coloured yellow and orange), organised by Philip, so we could all recognise each other when we gathered at the Queen's Head! Each year we have met for lunch in a suitable venue in Brighton, visited something interesting (e.g. the Aquarium) in the afternoon, then met for afternoon tea and an evening drink.

In 1998 a joint GALHA and SLAGO party was held at the London Lighthouse, with 28 SLAGO members and 30 GALHA members attending. A donation was made to Lighthouse as a result of this. And in the following year the final of the SLAGO quiz was held at the Goose and Carrot (the renamed Horse & Jockey) in Wellesley Road, Croydon.

In August 1999 a successful SLAGO Sculpture Day was held at Neil Godfrey's sculpture park in Godstone, with over eighty attending.

In the same year, Ross Burgess and his partner Roger held the first bonfire party was held in their garden in Purley, which continued each year until the bottom of their garden was sold off—no, not to fairies! It is still a very pleasant garden, the venue for our annual garden party or "Mardi on the Grass" in August—now the main SLAGO event of the year and much enjoyed by all. Many thanks to Roger and Ross for all their hard work organising this.

Conference time

Another successful thing SLAGO set up was two conferences, the first in 1995 at MCC Balham, chaired by Peter Robins, and the second in 1999 at the Bread & Roses, organised by Roger and Ross.

At the first one each group set out how they were progressing and really it was just a useful idea sharing and information giving event. Everyone agreed it had been a very worthwhile occasion.

The second conference put forward various ideas for the different groups to consider, such as how we could persuade more women and young people to join the groups, and how we should promote ourselves better. Peter Robins, who gave the main speech, stressed that diversity was important and useful. He felt that SLAGO should set up a working party to consider the best inter-group social activities in the future. Terry Murphy, chairing the discussion that followed, identified the lack of provision for youth, for ethnic minorities and for lesbians as areas in which we were nearly all collectively seriously failing. Probably still true today.

Unbelievably 17 groups attended the second conference (as far as we know, only the ones in italics are still in existence today): *CAGS, CHE*, Croydon Friend, Croydon Lesbian & Gay Forum, KRAGS, Magnet, Lewisham Gay Alliance, Libertines, *LMG, Marypad*, North London Gay Alliance, Pinks Down South, Pimpernel, Polari (replaced by Age of Diversity), *Redhill Area Gay Society, SLG*, Sunday-at-Two.

The conference also discussed the use of the (then) pioneering SLAGO website used later by many of the individual groups. Ross was working hard to set it up and continues to keep everything updated now.

Liaison Meetings and the website

Liaison meetings have been held every three months for the last fifteen years and various events are selected from the individual groups' programmes for the other groups to support. We all feel that the friendships we have formed have been mutually beneficial and useful.

Just for the record, the following groups were paid-up members of SLAGO, for all or some of the period from 1997 to 2002: CAGS, CAGY, Croydon Friend, GAGS, Hiking Dykes, KRAGS, Libertines, LMG, Magnet, MCC South London, Pimpernel, RAGS, SLG, Sunday-at-Two.

The SLAGO website at **www.slago.org.uk** contains a description of SLAGO and the full text of the SLAGO Agreement (effectively SLAGO's constitution) plus links to all the current member groups' home pages (some of which are maintained by SLAGO on behalf of the group in question). There's also a variety of useful information, including all the papers from the 1999 Conference. But the most useful part is the current programme, which lists forthcoming SLAGO events, plus any other events that member groups have asked us to publicise.

CAGS   CHE   South London Gays

3F (LGCM London)   MCC South London   SLAGO

Chapter Twenty-Eight
Courage UK 1988–

by Jeremy Marks

Courage UK is not to be confused with Courage RC, a Roman Catholic ministry, based in New York and committed to promoting celibacy

Jeremy Marks

A Christian Community

The ministry of Courage UK was founded in 1988, and was always intended to provide a safe place for lesbian and gay Christians who were "struggling to overcome" their homosexuality. The ministry began with a profound sense of personal calling (as a priestly role). My local church was very supportive and before long several wonderful key people joined me, supporting the ministry in important ways that enabled it to operate.

In the first place we offered regular support group meetings, which we still do. Only months later this developed to become a Christian community with several houses available for people to live in with us.

Several committed co-workers sold their homes to buy bigger houses to facilitate having a number of people to stay and share life in community.

All who approached Courage came from conservative evangelical or Roman Catholic Christian backgrounds. They all came from churches that taught that you could not be gay and Christian. Many of us bought into the pop-psychology of the time which suggested that homosexuality was indicative of a kind of "arrested development" resulting from having grown up in a home where mother was domineering and controlling, and father was largely absent—emotionally if not physically, thereby failing as an important role model (especially for their sons), who therefore grew up with a deep need for a father figure, a longing that had become "eroticised". So we believed that homosexuality was fundamentally caused by a strong need for unconditional love and for good same-sex role models who would bond with us in a healthy way and enable us to "grow up" into what we believed was our natural God-given heterosexual orientation. (Such theories have largely been discredited today.)

As Christians, we tried to cope with our same-sex desires by making a distinction between orientation (which we could not help) and practice (which was sin)—based on the kind of thinking that "God loves the sinner but hates the sin". We all determined to live a celibate life, and sought to "overcome" what we saw as a deviant desire, through healing prayer and by living as open and accountable members of the Christian community.

Being gay myself, I had already struggled with this for many years, in spite of much Christian counselling, psychotherapy, deliverance ministry and healing prayer—all to no avail. After all those years of experience one thing still seemed to be missing—and that was an experience of community life with other Christians, with whom you could be honest and open about life's struggles, and where you could find unconditional love. Courage was founded as part of a local church that set out to be that warm open Christian community which we all felt the need of. Our community houses provided a place where gay men (and one or two women) could live together and work out their Christian discipleship in a community setting.

Although any community life brings its challenges—just trying to relate to one another in a loving way—overall it was a great time; we felt a new sense of hope, common purpose and warm Christian fellowship. And

211

because we were gay, at last we felt free of the hidden guilt and shame we had all suffered as a result of the attitudes we had experienced in our homophobic society and churches. Even if we "fell" sexually, we felt free to confess and receive understanding and forgiveness with prayer support from our brothers and sisters in the community.

Jeremy Marks' recent book
Exchanging the Truth of God for a Lie

Nothing Had Changed

Our understanding was always that any kind of homosexual expression was sin—we were all agreed on that teaching from our churches.

All went well, more or less, until gradually the people who had come to us (from all over the world) reached the point where they had to go home. Leaving behind that loving and supportive community exposed the truth—that nothing had actually changed in their orientation at all. So they began to feel all the more alone, wondering what this experience of total dedication to Christ could have meant if it had not led to the change we all felt sure would come—especially when graduates of our discipleship programme found that the temptations to desire and seek a same-sex partnership were as strong and deeply-rooted as ever. Many lost their faith as a result; some became deeply depressed to the point of despair; some even became suicidal. As a pastor committed to helping people grow in their faith, I found the situation quite heart-breaking.

In the meantime, I had got married (in 1991) as a "step of faith". But even though I was always committed to obeying the will of God (as I perceived it), it was not long before I realised that nothing had changed my orientation, a fact that was just as difficult for my wife as for me. I was able to lead a faithful and celibate life, but mainly because I found value and affirmation in running the ministry. However, for others who married and did not have that kind of encouragement, divorce almost inevitably followed eventually (with just a few exceptions amongst those of us brought up with a very duty-orientated mindset).

Steering a Middle Course

By the mid-1990s, we'd had to close our residential houses, for various reasons (not least of those being the fact that the project had become more or less insolvent). Increasingly I felt that not only had our vision not been fulfilled, but worse—we had set people up with a tremendous expectation for healing based on a false hope, a specious illusion—that deliverance from unwanted same-sex desires would come if only we were prepared to struggle hard enough and for long enough. Seeing the experience of other ministries, especially those in the USA which had been going for much longer, made me gradually realise that we were never going to see our vision fulfilled. Increasingly I could see that the only people who were doing at all well were those who had come to the point of accepting that they were gay, and found a same-sex partner. The majority became more and more dysfunctional in life, as long as they suppressed what I eventually realised was their/our true sexuality.

For a while, we tried to steer a middle road where we recognised that a change of orientation was not going to happen. We encouraged celibacy and the development of close same-sex friendships—of a non-sexual kind. But this proved impracticable for most people; we completely underestimated the natural strength of desire we all have for the sexual consummation of a relationship with someone we love.

Meeting a group in the United States called Evangelicals Concerned, a long-running theologically conservative group that was, nevertheless, totally affirming of same-sex partnerships, helped me to see that this move, theologically, was both possible and entirely appropriate for gay Christians. In writing an article for LGCM magazine in 2000, to share my change of approach (a radical change for evangelical Christians), I had to go public about our new views. Consequently I lost fellowship with and support from most evangelical churches that had previously approved our "ex-gay" stance. But this freed me to be more open and candid about what I now believe—that God fully supports same-sex partnerships.

A Public Apology

In June 2005, I was invited by Peterson Toscano and the Soulforce group in the USA to join a conference called "Beyond ex-gay" where, alongside other former "ex-gay" ministry leaders, I made a public apology for our "ex-gay" work and all the damage it has done to gay people over the years. In my defence, I must say that I had endeavoured to follow the teachings of the conservative church—and all who had come to us needed to make the same journey—for none of us were able to embrace a fully gay-affirming perspective until we'd exhausted the "ex-gay" theories and discovered what is right in the sight of God for ourselves.

Jeremy Marks, Courage, September 2009

Chapter Twenty-Nine
The Barnet Group 1994–

The Barnet group was founded in 1994. Early venues included the Bull and Butcher in Whetstone and a room in Barnet College. These were followed by a Portakabin at the back of the Old Bull Arts Centre in Barnet High Street, which was called Studio Two.

The Old Bull Arts Centre, Barnet

From there they went to what everyone agrees was their most popular meeting place ever, the King George—further up the High Street towards Hadley. The management there was very welcoming and allotted the group their own area in the downstairs bar but with a room upstairs available for special occasions. The group met there for three years from the beginning of 1997. In fact on a Thursday night gays outnumbered the other customers, and the group was so popular that numbers often reached forty.

Quizzes and sometimes shows were put on by members in the upstairs room, including members revealing their talents in singing, dancing and even stripping! They used to have wonderful Christmas parties at the George, at which attendance often reached sixty, and in the summer barbecues were held in the garden there.

The former King George in Barnet High Street

Speakers over the years included Peter Tatchell and Stephen Twigg, the first MP to come out, as well as a leader of the Metropolitan Community Church and someone from the Happiness Project telling members how to be happy.

Most memorable outings included a visit (jointly with the Harrow Group) to the Houses of Parliament where they were shown around by Stephen Twigg—who was actually made an honorary member of the group—and a holiday weekend to Blackpool which was by all accounts enormous fun, with over twenty members attending.

Everything was fine at the George until the management changed. The new manager decided to renovate the whole pub and the Group lost the use of both the cosy corner and the upstairs room. For a while the Group used to meet in the main bar of the Crown and Anchor, a pub set right in the centre of Barnet opposite the big church. They then moved down the hill to the Red Lion, the pub near to the Barnet Odeon, later returning to the Bull and Butcher, Whetstone. (By the way at all these venues the Group met on a Thursday evening).

There was a serious side to the Group too, with committee members getting involved in forums with police, victim support and local health authorities at Hendon Town Hall. For Gay History Month an exhibition was put on at the Church House Museum in Greyhound Hill, also in Hendon (which is part of the London Borough of Barnet).

Sorties have also been made onto the North London gay scene, notably a Christmas lunch put on for the Group at the White Hart, Tottenham Hale.

The Group has changed its name several times, although its most popular name was probably BUGLE which is believed to stand for Barnet Ultimate Gay and Lesbian Experience!

It is hoped that in spite of recent setbacks the Group will soon recover the great successes of the past.

The Crown and Anchor (left), opposite Barnet Church

Our thanks to Royston of Mill Hill and Colin of Edgware for their help in putting this interesting account together. Ed.

Chapter Thirty
South London Gays 1995–

by Terry Murphy

Perhaps the last London gay group to be formed in the twentieth century was SLG.

On 12 November 1994 the 21st birthday party of the Wimbledon Area Gay Society (WAGS) was held in the King's Head pub in Colliers Wood. The party itself was highly successful, attended by almost 100 people, both existing and former WAGS members. However it was becoming increasingly clear that the group was in a state of steady decline.

The main focus of WAGS had been its weekly Wednesday meetings in the William Morris Hall, Wimbledon, but attendances had been falling for some time. The Hall itself was uninviting; visitors were confronted with old lino flooring, uncomfortable canvas and metal chairs and a drab room in need of decoration. It was difficult to sustain a high interest programme. The task of arranging an event there every week was putting a strain on the committee (of only four people) and the group was failing to attract or retain new members. Indeed, membership of WAGS had fallen to just over 20.

Financially, the group was also facing a potential problem. The meeting room was costing £10 to hire each week and this (together with the cost of a contact phone line) had been financed over several years by a grant of £650 per annum from Merton Council—Conservative controlled and reputedly one of the most right-wing in the country! After the Labour Party won control of the Council in 1994, they initiated a grants review, which resulted in advice to WAGS that its grant would cease. (Ironically much of the grant had in fact been going indirectly to Merton Labour Party since they owned the William Morris Hall.) The group was therefore faced with an imminent shortage of funding.

This decline in the fortunes of the group prompted a major review by the WAGS committee of its organisation and direction, since it was clear that the group was heading for eventual extinction—which has been the fate of many other local gay groups throughout the country. Fortunately for the group, it was helped by a stroke of good fortune.

It had always been very difficult to find reasonably priced and comfortable meeting rooms but WAGS certainly needed a change from William Morris Hall. Out of the blue, the committee were approached by the owners of a new gay pub in Clapham, who were keen to attract gay community groups. The WAGS Committee visited the Clockhouse pub in Clapham Park Road in August 1995 and it was just what they were looking for. The paint was hardly dry in the upstairs meeting room—newly decorated, spacious and light—it was ideal venue to re-launch the group, especially having a bar downstairs. Also, it was completely free! The pub made no charge for any non-profit-making gay group.

It was also decided to get away from the onus of weekly meetings. One meeting at the Clockhouse would take place each month (with a major emphasis on having a visiting speaker) and this would be supplemented by a varied programme of events, including days out, theatre and cinema visits, meals out and events in members' homes and also badminton and tennis matches. It was originally envisaged that members would develop informal networks for those with common interests, who could arrange meetings and events among themselves. However this did not develop and all activities were centrally organised by the committee.

Communication with members would also be streamlined. Instead of the time-consuming production of a booklet every two months containing events, articles and photos, the group decided to keep it simple—a double-sided bulletin containing the programme for the month with a few brief items of extra news or information. On the other hand more effort was put into publicity by way of leaflets and information placed on community notice boards and sent to local newspapers and the gay press.

The final task in the re-launch of the group was to find a new name. Several options were considered but the one which stood out was South London Gays. It was concise and reflected the catchment area more accurately than "Wimbledon Area" (although SLG has since attracted members from all over London, Surrey, Essex, Kent and beyond)

With everything in place, the official launch of SOUTH LONDON GAYS took place on Wednesday 13 September 1995 at its first monthly meeting at the Clockhouse pub. The speaker at the meeting was Terry Sanderson, who addressed issues covered in his then recently published book *Media Watch*. He was soon followed in November by Peter Tatchell who opened a discussion on the theme "Equal rights are not enough; assimilation versus emancipation".

At the same time, a social programme quickly developed starting with a coach trip to Eton College, followed by a visit to Bloolips at the Drill Hall Theatre. Cinema visits, pub evenings and events in members' homes soon followed and a badminton group was also established. Membership steadily grew to a viable number to sustain a lively and attractive group.

Tony writes about the SLG tennis group:

The tennis group within SLG started in 1997, with matches being played at the courts on Clapham Common. Around the year 2000, parking restrictions were introduced in that area so we decided to move down to Haydons Recreation Ground in South Wimbledon. This was an ideal venue because there was free parking space, plus both tube and train stations nearby, and we had quite a thriving group of players.

Unfortunately in 2003 the local council decided to hire the tennis courts out to motor cyclist trainers, probably because it was more profitable, and we lost the use of the courts. By coincidence the badminton group hit similar problems: they had met every Saturday afternoon at Wimbledon Leisure Centre in Latimer Road, but that facility was shut down as the courts were being turned into a gym—presumably also because it was more profitable.

Since then the SLG tennis group has been at John Innes Park in Mostyn Road (near South Merton station and just about in walking distance of Morden tube)—a delightful and historic location.

Standards are not amazingly high but we always manage to enjoy several good games! We meet alternate Tuesday mornings from March to November, and are keen to recruit new members. Maybe you used to play when younger and would consider having another try? If yes, you will be made most welcome.

220

Back to Terry:

Although we have changed our venue to the pleasant Bread & Roses pub in Clapham Manor Street for the monthly meetings (2009), the basic format for South London Gays has remained the same for the past 15 years. The main focus is on the monthly meetings (second Tuesday monthly except August) with guest speakers, who have included local MPs, gay writers, religious representatives, journalists, and members of lesbian and gay political groups.

This has been supplemented by a wide range of social activities—between eight and ten per month. Although primarily a social group, SLG has also been involved in various letter-writing campaigns on gay issues over many years and is involved in joint events with other gay groups in London and Surrey.

Membership of the group in 2009 was about 80 and it costs £7 per year (£5 unwaged) to join (it's not obligatory to live in South London!) Those interested in joining are invited to get further details by writing to: SLG, PO Box 243, London SW19 1XW or e-mail **slgnews@aol.com**. You can also view the website (hosted by SLAGO) at **www.slago.org.uk/slg**.

Bibliography

Some highly recommended titles for further reading

Batten, Rex   **Rid England of this Plague** (2006). A terrifying and vivid eye-witness account of the 1950s purge of homosexuals.

David, Hugh   **On Queer Street**: (1997). A Social History of British Homosexuality, 1895–1995.

Doorn, Jeffrey   **Slivers of Silver.** Poems by gay men and women, edited by Jeffrey Doorn and Adrian Risdon. Paradise Press. Also "Journey Round the Circle Line" in **Queer Haunts**, edited by G Abel-Watters.

Johnson, Malcolm   **Outside the Gate** (1994). The story of St Botolph's Church Aldgate, including their ministry both to the poor and to gays.

Marks, Jeremy   **Exchanging the Truth of God for a Lie** (2009). An evangelical Christian rethinks his views on homosexuality.

Power, Lisa   **No Bath but Plenty of Bubbles** (1995). An oral history of the Gay Liberation Front, 1970–1973.

Tatchell, Peter   **The Battle for Bermondsey** (1983). Peter explains his views on extra-parliamentary action, gay rights and a "new style" of MP which made him unacceptable to the Labour establishment.

Weeks, Jeffrey   **Coming Out** (Revised 1990). Homosexual politics in Britain from the 19th Century to the Present.

London CHE Groups in October 1976

* Barnet & Brent
* Bexley-Dartford
  Bloomsbury (Group 4)
* Bromley
  Chiswick
* Croydon (Group 7)
  East London
  Enfield
  Feltham
  Guildford *(just outside!)*
* Harrow
* Kingston
* Lewisham
* London Monday (Group 10)
* Marypad (Group 6)
  North London
  Piccadilly
* Southwark-Lambeth
* Streatham
* Wandsworth-Richmond
* West End
  Westminster
* Young London

We are grateful to the Hall-Carpenter archives for supplying this information.

* *The starred groups have a section on them in this book.*

Abbreviations used in this Book

2LGA	Lewisham Lesbian & Gay Association
3F	Third Fellowship (LGCM London group)
BADGERS	Bexley And District Gay Educational & Recreational Society
BUGLE	Barnet Ultimate Gay & Lesbian Experience
CHE	Campaign for Homosexual Equality
CAGS	Croydon Area Gay Society
CAGY	Croydon Area Gay Youth
CHEK	CHE Kingston
CHELIC	CHE London Information Centre
CHERP	CHE Richmond-Putney
CHEWEG	CHE West End Group
EGG	Ealing Gay Group
GAGS	Guildford Area Gay Society
GCO	Gay Community Organisation
GALHA	Gay and Lesbian Humanist Association
GLF	Gay Liberation Front
HGU	Harrow Gay Unity
ILEA	Inner London Education Authority
JGLG	Jewish Gay and Lesbian Group
KRAGS	Kingston and Richmond Area Gay Society
LGBT	Lesbian, gay, bisexual and transgendered
LGCM	Lesbian and Gay Christian Movement
LLGC	London Lesbian and Gay Centre
LMG	London Monday Group
MCC	Metropolitan Community Church
NWLLG	North West London Lesbians and Gays
RAGS	Redhill Area Gay Society
SAGG	Streatham Area Gay Group
SK	St Katharine's Group
SLAGO (SAGO)	Surrey & London Association of Gay Organisations
SLG	South London Gays
ULU	University of London Union
WAGS	Wimbledon Area Gay Society

Geography of the London Gay Groups

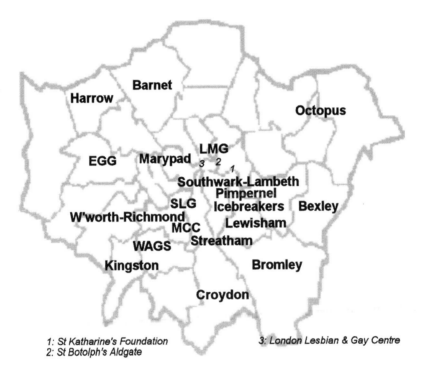

Harrow   Barnet   Octopus

EGG   Marypad   LMG
3 2 1
Southwark-Lambeth
Pimpernel
SLG   Icebreakers   Bexley
W'worth-Richmond   Lewisham
MCC
WAGS   Streatham
Kingston   Bromley
Croydon

1: St Katharine's Foundation   3: London Lesbian & Gay Centre
2: St Botolph's Aldgate

*Our thanks to Michael Ouen Brown
and to Ross Burgess for producing this map.*

Some Web Addresses

Many of the groups mentioned in this book have their own websites:

3F (LGCM Central London)	*www.slago.org.uk/3f*
Barnet Lesbian & Gay Group	*www.barnetgay.com*
Bromley Gay & Bi Men's Group	*www.slago.org.uk/bromleygaymensgroup*
CAGS (Croydon Area Gay Society	*www.cags.org.uk*
CHE (Campaign for Homosexual Equality)	*www.c-h-e.org.uk*
Courage UK	*www.courage.org.uk*
Ealing Gay Group	*www.ealinggaygroup.org.uk*
GALHA (Gay and Lesbian Humanist Association)	*www.galha.org*
Hall-Carpenter Archives	*http://hallcarpenter.tripod.com*
Jewish Gay and Lesbian Group (JGLG)	*www.jglg.org.uk*
LGBT History Month	*www.lgbthistorymonth.org.uk*
LGCM (Lesbian & Gay Christian Movement)	*www.lgcm.org.uk*
LMG (formerly London Monday Group)	*www.slago.org.uk/lmg*
London Friend	*www.londonfriend.org.uk*
MCC East London	*www.mcceastlondon.org.uk*
MCC North London	*www.mccnorthlondon.org*
MCC South London	*www.mccsouthlondon.co.uk*
Octopus	*www.octopusgroup.org.uk*
Quest	*www.questgaycatholic.org.uk*
Schools OUT	*www.schools-out.org.uk*
SLAGO (Surrey & London Association of Gay Organisations)	*www.slago.org.uk*
SLG (South London Gays)	*www.slago.org.uk/slg*
The Transport Group	*www.transportgroup.freeserve.co.uk*

For possible corrections and updates to this book see *www.slago.org.uk/oots.htm* and for gay groups throughout London see LGBT London *www.lgbtlondon.com* —and for LGBT history generally see the new wiki at *www.lgbthistoryuk.org*

Index

Page numbers in italics indicate illustrations. Numbers in bold indicate major chapters or sections.